OXFORD

MATTHEW RICE
OXFORD

WHITE
LION
PUBLISHING

PETER RICE 1928 — 2015
PAT ALBECK 1930 — 2017

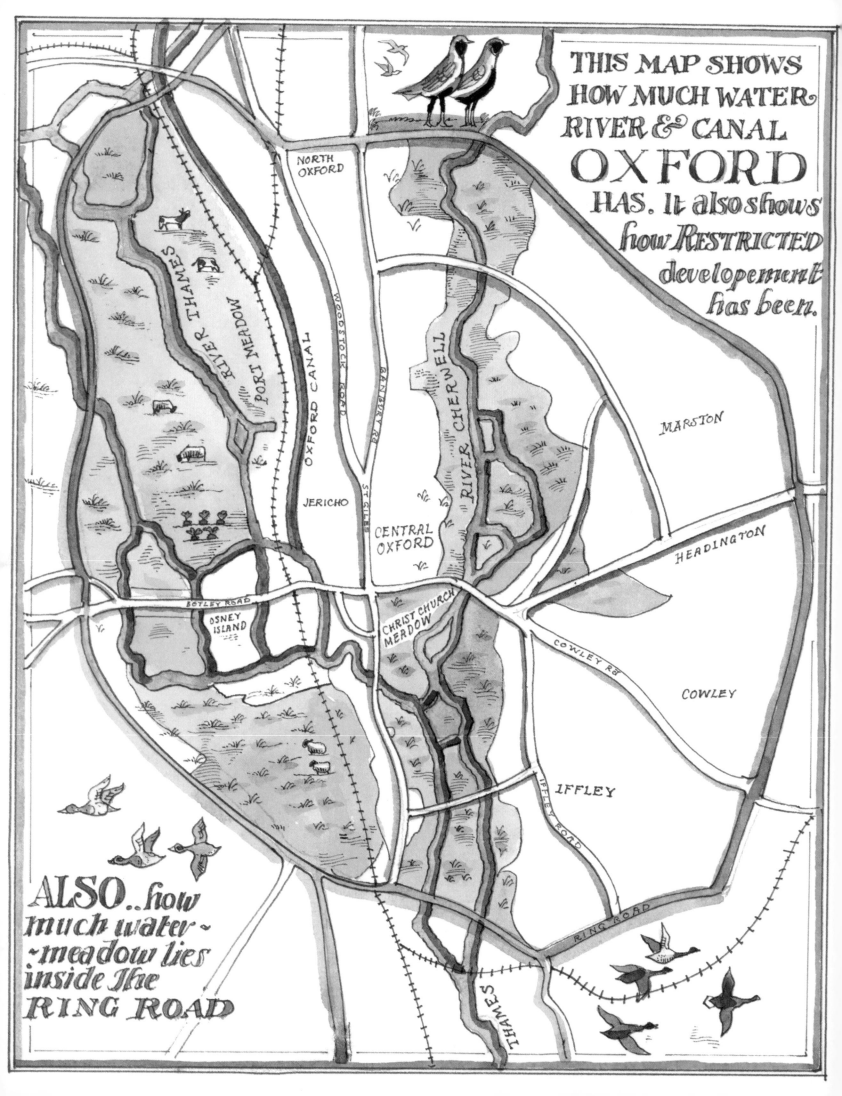

THIS MAP SHOWS HOW MUCH WATER RIVER & CANAL OXFORD HAS. It also shows how RESTRICTED developement has been.

ALSO..how much water-meadow lies inside the RING ROAD

NORTH OXFORD

RIVER THAMES

PORT MEADOW

OXFORD CANAL

WOODSTOCK ROAD

BANBURY RD

ST GILES

JERICHO

CENTRAL OXFORD

RIVER CHERWELL

MARSTON

HEADINGTON

BOTLEY ROAD

OSNEY ISLAND

CHRIST CHURCH MEADOW

COWLEY RD

COWLEY

IFFLEY

IFFLEY ROAD

RING ROAD

THAMES

INTRODUCTION

Like Venice, Paris, Bath or Edinburgh, people talk specifically about the buildings of Oxford. They are an inalienable part of the city and the university's attraction and reputation. Plenty of cities have other characteristics that occlude the bricks and mortar: Liverpool's music and the Mersey, Glasgow's wild living, or Stoke-on-Trent's potteries, but Oxford's strapline of 'the dreaming spires' ties the place inextricably to its buildings. There are few other places in the world to contend with the centre of the city for unbroken architectural beauty and interest. Oxford escaped the blight of bombing in the Second World War. Like Venice, Florence or Rome, its status as one of Western culture's most complex and variegated collections of buildings, combined with the relative absence of buildings of industrial or military significance, gave it a safe pass to escape the extreme damage wrought on so many less fortunate British and European cities.

It is the university, with eight hundred years of clever men and women concentrated in what would otherwise be a middle sized county town, that has created Oxford's status as an architectural sculpture park. One outstanding exemplar follows another in an area so small that there is barely room for the everyday. Competing hunger by the university and individual colleges for city centre land has all but erased domestic architecture. The few gabled timber framed houses that remain, some in recognisable form and others cased in stucco in imitation of their masonry clad neighbours, owe their survival to the antiquarian enthusiasms of various college fellows. The colleges have, in general, gained ownership of those houses which until a century ago were fated to be razed to the ground to facilitate

one grand architectural spectacle or another. Most excitingly for anybody at all interested in buildings the long stretch of expenditure on beams, tiles, slates, rubble, Ashlar, woodwork, leadwork, glass and sculpture means that Oxford is like a living encyclopaedia of English architecture. This book divides that corpus of work into five parts: monastic and medieval, baroque, Georgian, Gothic revival and modern. These chapters in the city's architectural history really reflect the periods in which the university and, subsequently, the town itself felt the impetus to invest.

Other moments are less well represented. The period immediately after the dissolution of the monasteries, the Whig ascendency in the mid eighteenth century, the Regency and the agricultural depression of the 1880s all had depressing effects on both student numbers and on the funds available for grand projects. In contrast was the change in the profile of scholars over the centuries, from poor clever students destined to be clerks in the great monastic orders to entitled sons of the gentry and aristocracy. The expectations of the latter group, both in terms of comfort and in levels of general architectural sophistication, brought pressures to bear on colleges intending to recruit from that particularly wealthy section of society. The obvious solution was to transform the accommodation that colleges could offer, abandoning the austerity of shared bedrooms and cramped studies in favour of elegant chambers with two or three rooms and space for a servant. These sets of rooms characterise the defining elegance of grand colleges like Magdalen, Queen's and Christ Church: long ranges of calmly repeating windows and columns or pilasters, simple parapets and balustrades and, of course, an absence

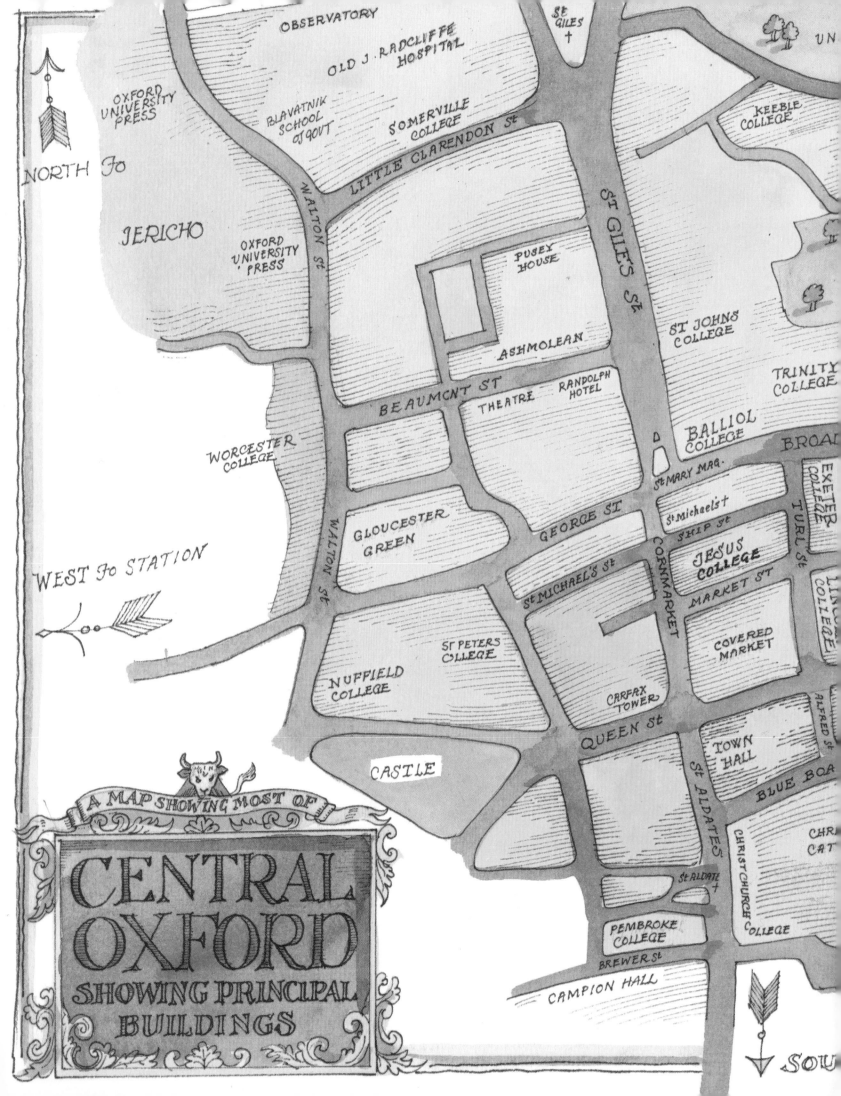

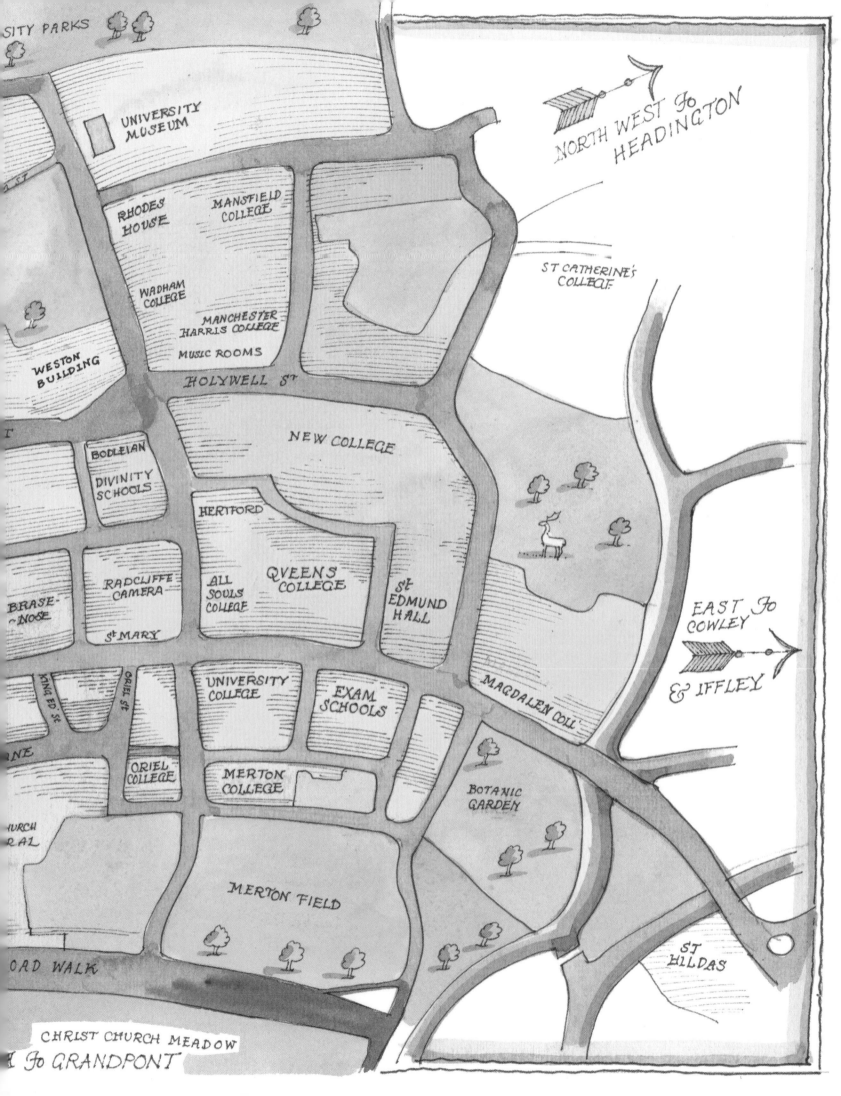

of any Gothic ornament. They are a mirror held up to the great country houses being designed and built for the very families whose sons were now the desired undergraduates of the growing university. Those tastes, and those of the fellows of these institutions, were intensely influenced by the Grand Tour. This rite of passage, a trip often of two or three years duration to Southern Europe, was, by the eighteenth century, fast becoming a *sine qua non* of the education of aristocratic or aspirational young men. By crossing the alps with the assistance of bold mountain men, before then being transferred from rumbling wagon to 'Swiss Chair' to navigate the precipitous passes as St Bernard turns into that of San Bernardino, or Mont Blanc into Monte Bianco, the future cognoscenti of enlightenment Britain arrived in the balmy Mediterranean. Often accompanied by a teacher cum guide, the *jeunesse dorée* of the developing North imbibed wholesale the sun-soaked efflorescence of the Italian Renaissance. Drifting from the moss gathering stones of the ancients and the Roman inspired gardens and palazzi of popes and cardinals, to the set piece exemplars of the masters of classicism and the baroque like Alberti, Bramante, Palladio and Bernini, these newly opened eyes assimilated a whole new culture and brought it, or an appreciation of it, back to Britain and to Oxford.

While a university town is one with a large and self-consciously elite population of young men (no women were admitted to the university until the end of the nineteenth century) there is also a backdrop of non-university buildings in Oxford. The town predates the university by half a millennium and its early pattern of parishes is still clear from its churches, even if some have now been converted

for academic use. There were sixty buildings or complexes of buildings under the care and use of the Catholic Church in 1546, but, by the beginning of the nineteenth century, a mere eleven of these were in regular religious use by the Anglican Church, many serving as college chapels. However non-university and secular Oxford remains; no more striking contrast exists than that between two of the streets that meet at Carfax in the centre of Oxford. The High Street, curving for four hundred yards towards Magdalen Bridge is a stage set of palaces, monastic gatehouses, baroque columns and towers to rival the grandest in the country. Along this street, when it is not a slow moving river of appreciative tourists, the university is on display. Students, either beetling and earnest, or floating on a benign cloud of entitlement, wander from college to library, return from rugby or hockey matches in sports kit or, while deconstructing colonialism or Love Island, lean against the same masonry that has supported their predecessors for centuries. Dons scurry to the pleasures of the senior common rooms and North Oxford mothers, whose children are happily installed in some of the best schools in the country, bustle with recyclable bags and baskets to flirt with butchers or croon at the rocket and radicchio in the covered market. It is rarefied, sustained and made real by the living presence of a vast medieval university structure. But turn right into Cornmarket and the visitor might be in Warwick or Swindon. Oxford flies the colours of a South Midlands market town. An utterly different population appears to be about its business (they are, of course, mainly the very same people) as from Snappy Snaps and Subway to Schuh, from WH Smith to Macdonald's, the fabric of town Oxford, with its factories, schools and railway stations, is here in the ascendency. The homeless and the musically aspirational busk in doorways and shoppers from out-of-town visit the gloomy Westgate shopping centre (once possibly the worst building in Oxford, but now mercifully rebuilt with a contemporary glaze of superficial sophistication). But while Cornmarket, Queen Street and, to a lesser extent, George Street are part of Oxford, they are the bit of the city that is least characteristic and so least interesting to visitors without shopping bags.

This nearly unique situation — a city centre where commerce is secondary — means that the colleges, churches, museums, pubs and schools are in the ascendancy. Oxford is a major tourist destination and, outside term time, legions of French children, Italian students and Chinese or Korean ladies obediently following their banner fluttering guides fill the city. Over the swirling Solomonic columns of St Mary's, the pie crust Gothic glamour of All Souls, or the orderly classical domed drum of the Radcliffe Camera, these tour groups clash adoring eyes with smaller groups of private visitors or select teams lead by a desperate looking guide shamed by his shiny Mad hatter's costume, or a smiling undergraduate hurrying to get his £40 and get back to work. A song of adoration of the genuinely oddly shaped Sheldonian Theatre leads to explanatory notes on Michael Black's giant emperors' heads and then on to the dramatic chiaroscuro of the Clarendon building. The Belgian family's breath is plucked from them as they turn the corner into Radcliffe Square, which even the most stone-weary, culture-sated aesthete sees for the first time with utter astonishment. It is a *coup de théâtre*, a totally unplanned but beautifully conceived square made up of equally unlikely bedfellows. A Gothic church staring down at an enlightenment library and, behind them, appears a series of dramatic backdrops from operas set in every period, held together by a floor cloth of golden cobbles. Whether glistening in a rainy November midnight, glowing in a winter sunset or ghostly in the September mists it is profoundly atmospheric, but it can also take the hard midday summer sun, where its varied detailing provides a dictionary of architectural terms of unbeatable breadth.

Incidentally, the cobbles in Radcliffe Square prove that architectural effect is not all about elevations and ground plans. The materials employed beneath our feet are of equal significance. We walk, if we are to avoid unseemly tumbles, looking down as well as forward or up. If the ground is brute modern, cracked black asphalt or concrete paving slabs, then the total *mise en scène* is compromised. In this stage-set like composition, the cobbles are an essential component.

Oxford is an architectural *tour de force* but it is one that is made up of seven hundred years of the best building. It is the product of the best materials, the best architects and builders, and the best clients. Other great architectural compositions, like the Escorial near Madrid or Haussmann's Paris, had a single great Prospero, or, as in an Italian city state like Mantua, a family of prosperous patrons, but Oxford's buildings were commissioned by hundreds of the cleverest men in Europe. They still are.

High status projects attract good architecture, or, at any rate, enable good architects to express themselves fully and to employ the best materials and craftsmen for the job. In Britain as a whole the hierarchy of building changed abruptly from ecclesiastical to secular following Henry VIII's break with Rome and the dissolution of the monasteries. The focus of excellence moved to the houses and palaces of the 'new men', those who had gained most from the seismic reordering of English society, and those men whose efforts had been devoted to the last great burst of English Gothic as exemplified by King's College Chapel or St. George's Chapel at Windsor Castle, were re-directed to the secular palaces of the 'new men' and on to the prodigy houses of the sixteenth century. In fact, not only were resources heading in a new direction, but the actual stones which monastic Britain had been built out of were employed again in the houses of the 'new men'. But, in this moment of great dynamism and innovation, the great universities held their breath. There was an immediate fall in student numbers at the university and, while the status of these often renamed institutions continued to be high, the new foundations chose to adapt and amend rather than to undertake ambitious new projects.

By the turn of the century Oxford was once again the intellectual centre of Britain and, under the Stuart monarchs, it became an integral setting for court life. Oxford's centrality was at its clearest when Charles I moved the court and government to the city when disloyal London was in the hands of Oliver Cromwell. From 1642-1645 the Stuart court moved lock, stock, and barrel to Oxford. The colleges proved to be ideal settings for this rival but legitimate parliament. The King himself moved into Christ Church while his privy council met at nearby Oriel College. An arsenal was established at All Souls and gunpowder was stored at New College. The court was accommodated in residential terms in Jesus, Pembroke and St John's. This

lasted until 1646 when, after a third siege, the King fled to London and Oxford was taken by the parliamentarians under Fairfax.

In architectural output the Interregnum proved unsurprisingly arid, but the Restoration brought the classical language in baroque clothes to town. Wren, who had already held the Savilian Chair of Astronomy at Oxford, first built the Sheldonian and, later, the North Tom Tower gate to Christ Church.

The period from the very end of the seventeenth century up until the middle of the eighteenth century – Sacheverell Sitwell's 'golden age' of British design in all fields from silver to great halls – is perhaps better represented in Oxford than anywhere else in the country. There is nowhere better to compare and contrast architectural styles without ever getting into the car.

As the university and its colleges grew so they built in subsequent styles and, as the classical supplanted the Gothic, so new ranges were thrown up in the new style to sit alongside their predecessors. The Gothic revival which dominated nineteenth-century British architecture was partly dreamt up in the city and it found powerful expression here in colleges, churches and the dramatically successful development of North Oxford from 1870 onwards.

Tempting as it would be to limit the selection of buildings illustrated here to those easily visible on any given day (indeed this would still make a glorious selection of the country's most lively and interesting buildings), doing so would risk omitting so much of the best. So here are some brief practical instructions. Parts of most colleges (except All Souls) are open at some point most days, but much

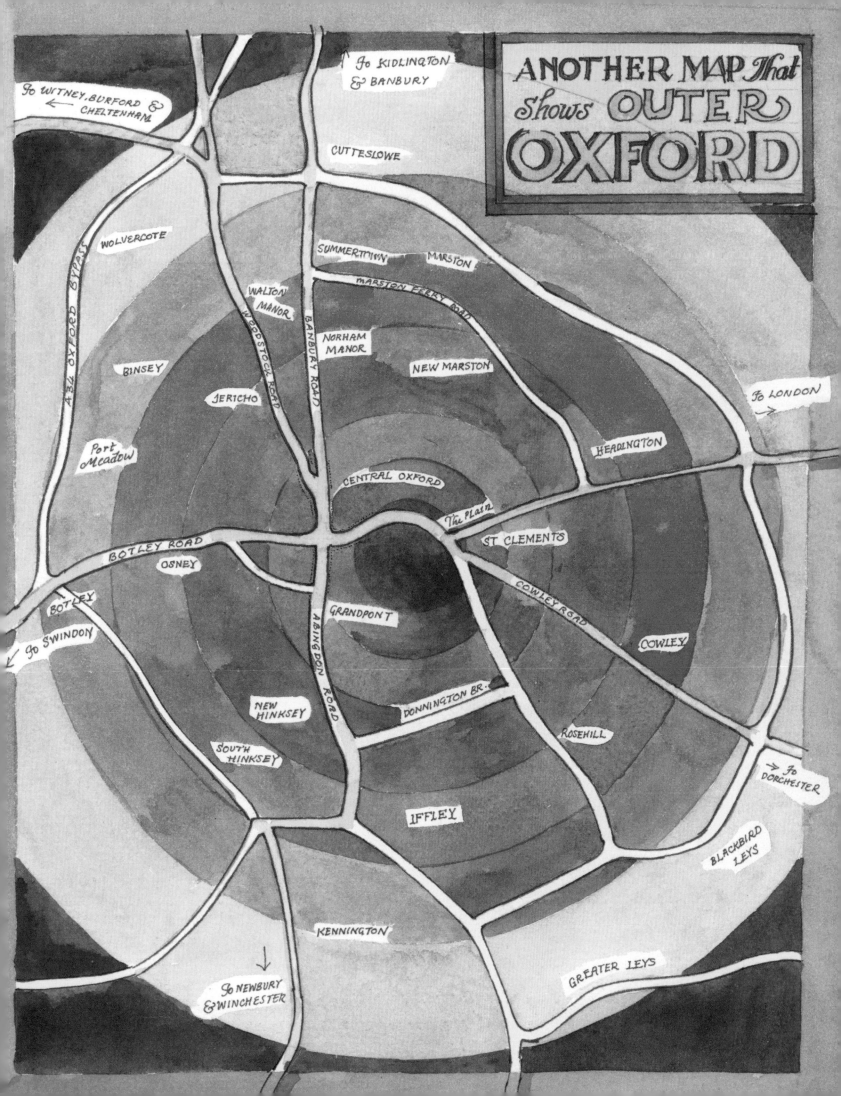

more is visible to the public on heritage open days in the first weekend of September each year. But when closed, the colleges are closed. Oxford porters are used to interlopers, and the tweediest and best informed are rigorously expelled along with the nosiest day trippers. Kind enquiries, or claims of false godchildren awaiting a visit, are treated with the same excoriating clarity and rejected. Some colleges like Magdalen sensibly charge for entry and they are consequently regularly open, while Christ Church Picture Gallery also keeps regular hours. In some ways this is, of course, an overcautious warning. The external elevations of most colleges, the towers and pinnacles visible at every turn, those churches not repurposed for college use, the two masterpiece museums of the Ashmolean and the Pitt Rivers, and the set piece spectacles of the High, St Giles and Radcliffe Square, as well as the more domestic scaled Merton Lane, are a button bursting feast of architectural ornament.

Around the world almost any town with a hundred yards of enclosed water is dubbed the Venice of the North, South, marshes, jungle, High Andes etc. It is not a title Oxford has ever needed (while San Antonio, Texas, for example, in my opinion does need a little help...) but, in fact, the confluence of two small rivers (the Windrush and the adolescent Thames) along with the presence of various lesser waterways and the Oxford canal makes water a significant element of the city. Rivers create a need for bridges, flood plains and waterfronts and, of course, access in the form of towpaths. The Thames is the leading man, thirty yards wide and at times fast flowing. It is a powerful presence at Christ Church and Worcester and, as it winds down to Iffley, it supports a thousand acres of inner city wildlife habitat. Otters and badgers twitch snouts along with classics dons, while herons and egrets float like feathered drones over the city. Oxford's ducks are ubiquitous. There are everyday mallards in the river and college gardens and more romantic teal and widgeon either in swirling flocks on Port Meadow or waddling along the riverbank in Christ Church Meadow. Sometimes one can see them hung neatly in little bunches outside the butchers in the covered market waiting to become delicious dinner for high table only...

Oxford is not a topographically interesting prospect.

It is its position as a city set in the meadows that defines its character. But, while it is built on gravel beds, good building stone is in relatively easy reach. Quarries were utilised either locally in Headington or further afield frequently using the river Windrush to get stone from the Taunton quarry near Burford. Later, stone from Clipsham in Northamptonshire, Portland in Dorset or Northern France was used for Oxford's buildings and, before flatbed lorries could fetch giant blocks of masonry from anywhere, it was the convenient and easily navigable Thames that provided the means of delivery. The movement of stone in medieval England was bafflingly difficult. There were no roads. The orderly pattern of die-straight stone-metalled roads established by the Romans would not be rivalled until the nineteenth century. The easy bouncing of the pneumatic tyre was half a millennium away which made transport bumpy to say the least, and the manufacturing effort involved in creating a single block of ashlar (that is a smooth faced stone used as a component of a building's elevation) is astonishing. The hours of chiselling that made up each door or window case are unthinkable in a modern consumer economy. Despite these difficulties, Oxford became a city of stone like its Cotswold neighbours. Unlike the next towns along on the Thames of Dorchester, Marlow and Henley, Oxford held brick at bay until the nineteenth century when, following its noble use in Keble College, it covered the city's outskirts with neat rows of artisan villas of the sort found from Sunderland to Southampton.

Old Oxford is a simple plan of a city, a plan that clearly shows its early Saxon and medieval shape, but so thrilling are its architectural decorations that it is hard to see past the individual buildings. Treats are also dense on the ground, alleys and lanes not excluded, so maps are useful. Some buildings, particularly important pre-Reformation monastic establishments, have disappeared without trace.

This book describes some of the city's best buildings, not as a tour guide and certainly not as a text book, but rather as a celebration and explanation of what, for residents, students or visitors from around the world, is a most compelling and extraordinary collection of buildings. It is, perhaps, the most important and complete built history of architecture in the country.

MONASTIC OXFORD

Early days to 1536

Medieval England was part of a global economy because its finances were inextricably linked with the outside world through the Roman Catholic Church. The monastic institutions of Oxford (in 1536 there were nine hundred) defined the city's intellectual culture. These institutions were formed by several different monastic orders including Benedictines, Augustinians, White, Grey and Blackfriars and, later, Carthusians and Franciscans. These monastic orders controlled a huge proportion of the productive farmland of Britain and thus the incomes deriving from those lands. The Benedictine abbey in nearby Abingdon, for example, possessed the sixth largest income of any estate in the country. While the power of the church was all but destroyed by Henry VIII in the 1530s, and he reapportioned the money and property of the hundreds of religious houses that he closed in great part to himself, those houses had been a significant power in the land for the previous half millennium. To be an abbot of a large monastic foundation was to play a part as powerful as that of a major secular magnate at court; indeed from the conquest onwards these posts were usually filled from the same small circle. William the Conqueror's brother Odo was Bishop of Bayeux, and he was one of many Norman grandees to take on the role of bishop, prior or abbot in the already powerful English Catholic Church after the Norman conquest.

These institutions were the recipients of frequent benefactions both in money and in kind, specifically in the form of property. Manors, or portions of landholdings, were made over to the church, swelling monastic property portfolios and coffers throughout the country. Some gifts accompanied appointments; others were more

straightforward investments in spiritual well-being. In a period when hell and purgatory were perceived as being as real as India or Cathay, investment to avoid visiting either destination was considered prudent, even essential. In effect, the church performed the function of current day insurance companies but with an unbreakable and lucrative monopoly. The methods by which this insurance might be effected were indulgences, pardons and the establishment of chantries (that is the engagement of a priest employed to say masses for the salvation of their deceased patron's soul). These spiritual insurance policies were massively beneficial financially for the Church and, along with legacies and gifts, allowed for the amassing of considerable institutional fortunes and, with those fortunes, the ability to undertake major building projects.

Ironically, despite the huge investment in stone, time and imaginative effort, the cataclysmic events of Henry VIII's break from Rome and the far reaching effects of the English Reformation have left us with little to show for all of this ecclesiastical wealth. The great abbeys of Rewley, Osney, Godstow and St Frideswide's were abolished, leaving only the last which was subsequently re-named as Christ Church cathedral. Similarly, the Blackfriars and the Carmelites established significant houses in a city that, by the thirteenth century, had become an important centre of learning.

Learning itself, and the emergence of England's two great universities, was predicated on the wealth and significance of the church. The principal recipients of this education were themselves bound for a life in holy orders either as priests or as the operators of canon law. The church legal system is now limited to what are generally arcane but hotly disputed

issues within the Anglican Church but, at best, marginal for most people in secular Britain. But, in the middle ages, church courts held sway over the lives of a large proportion of the country's population, due to the huge number of manors held by the monastic houses. This situation meant the church courts had to adjudicate in disputes relating to tenure, employment, marriages and inheritances, as well as the detailed legal structures which accompany a large and complicated conglomeration of property.

The existence and prosperity of the university, which was becoming a coherent entity by the end of the twelfth century, was partly accelerated by Henry II's ruling that English students should not continue to study at the university of Paris. This university was itself established as part of the church of Notre Dame, furnishing another example of the paramount importance of the Catholic Church in medieval Europe. By 1201 the post of 'magister scolarum Oxonie' was established, before changing to that of 'Chancellor' in 1214.

Ecclesiastical influence spread further into the fledgling university and so into the growing town of Oxford. Colleges were frequently established by prelates. Three separate Bishops of Winchester founded colleges, an indication of the importance of that position, first in precedence after the archbishoprics of Canterbury and York. William of Wykeham founded New College in 1379, William Waynflete (c.1398-1486) was founder of Magdalen (1458) and Richard Fox founded Corpus Christi College in 1517. Similarly, Exeter College was established in 1314 by Walter de Stapledon, Bishop of Exeter. Other institutions like Gloucester College (later Worcester College) and Blackfriars Hall were established directly by religious houses.

The monastic origin of the colleges is also evident from their physical layout. The specific combination of buildings – normally consisting of a chapel (here reduced from abbey church), a dining hall, a cloister, a dormitory and a library – is identical to that of any abbey or friary. The colleges would have felt instantly familiar to any clerics who moved to them from abbeys.

The university church of St Mary served as the university's council and meeting house from its earliest days. In 1320 a two-storey addition to the church was erected to the north. The vaulted room below was used for 'convocation' and the original university library was housed on the upper floor. The latter was also the result of an episcopal gift from Thomas Cobham, Bishop of Worcester. This university function was combined with its life as a parish church until the completion of Wren's Sheldonian Theatre in 1669.

In keeping with its growing significance, the town developed a close group of parish churches, some of Saxon origin and others with later Norman roots. While all this ecclesiastical energy was being expended the town of Oxford was also expanding. City walls, a castle, bridges, inns and houses were constructed alongside the abbeys, churches and colleges. Little of this civic building now survives, with only fragments of the city wall, occasionally incorporated into existing structures, still standing and, of course, the castle mound.

Medieval Oxford, a factory producing an educated caste of clerks and priests, was central to a country in which the Roman Catholic Church played such a dominant cultural and political role. But its role in the national picture was about to change abruptly with the first wave of the English Reformation.

MONASTIC OXFORD

SOUTH RANGE Worcester college (from the back)
(15). This is a remnant of its earlier existence as
GLOUCESTER College (until 1714, established as a
monastic establishment circa 1283)

DORMERS etc Gothicized in 18/19th CENTURY as Range
was heightened in 1824...GOTHIC ORNÉE...like Blaise Hamlet

Hall, MERTON College - This is in PART a really EARLY building first recorded in 1277 BUT re-modelled by Wyatt 1746-1813 and then neary totally REBUILT by Gilbert Scott 1811-1878 in 1872-74. DOOR is original with C13 ironwork

FRONT QUAD . CORPUS CHRISTI College built before 1517 when college founded. This Quad is paved (no velvet lawns for fellows' use only) This is what all QUADS once were like ...

South Elevation of Old Library. MOB QUAD · MERTON College
windows ⑭ if single ⑮ when double. The Earliest
complete Oxford Quad

GODSTOW ABBEY *Ruins*, a BENEDICTINE
Nunnery founded 1133. Little trace of the
Building remains except a walled
enclosure and small CHAPEL · early C16
Uffenbach writes in 1710 "Fair Rosamund,
mistress of Henry II has epitaph in the chapel
at Godstow. Almost in Ruins.."
She was Rosamund de Clifford, daughter
of a Marcher Lord born before 1150 died at
Godstow 1176

The CLOISTER of Magdalen College.. These doors and windows are in the interior walkway and gives visitors a strong feeling of monkish chat in Monastic oxford. The Cloister was built 1475-90. One of the other GOOD Things about This is that Magdalen is always open to the public - (you PAY..) so it is an easy opportunity to get inside one of the most BEAUTIFUL OXFORD COLLEGES.

GATEWAY go GLOUCESTER
College now WORCESTER College

The Passage of Buildings made along New college Lane and Queen's Lane is able to communicate a little of MEDIEVAL Oxford particularly atmospheric at Night.....
The Warden's BARN was built to store AGRICULTURAL produce from the surrounding College Landholdings.... 1402

Entrance To NEW COLLEGE on new college
Lane. This (says Pevsner) is the first oxford
Gate Tower late ⑭ .... Figures of the
founder William of Wykeham, Angel of
Annunciation and BVM in Niches

This Gate does <u>not</u> welcome VISITORS and
was built to keep out RIOTOUS townspeople

Similar GATE TOWER nearby. This
is The 4 Storey'd entrance to ALL
SOULS COLLEGE

ST Frideswide was a saxon Princess born about 650
She founded a priory but (according to the chronicler
William of Malmesbury (1095 - 1145) was pursued
as bride by the mercian King Algar but divine fate
spins him off his horse outside Oxford & his neck is
broken. she remains Abbess dying in 727

All that remains of what would have once been an
Impressive SHRINE to St FRIDESWIDE. In Christ
Church Cathedral once dedicated to her in
its entirety

CHRIST CHURCH CATHEDRAL · NAVE ARCADE C 1180

29

16 CENTURY DOORCASE at HERTFORD College (HART HALL until 1740) detail shows reading desk perhaps to inspire STUDIOUSNESS

REMAINS of The CLOISTER of WOLSEY'S CARDINAL COLLEGE begun 1525 . HIS FALL from Power in 1529 marked the end of This most grandiose project. The marked out Arches are monument to his overvaunting ambition... how the mighty are fallen...

FOOTING for front of CLOISTER

(16) DOORCASE at ST EDMUND HALL

WALL & TOWER at LONGWALL St · This is part of the boundary of Magdalen College and __not__ Part of The City wall - part of nearby NEW COLLEGE

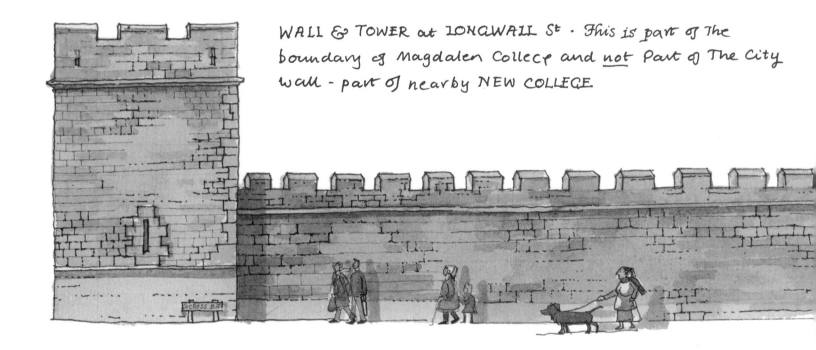

PARISH CHURCHES

Oxford's role as a university city means that many of the most architecturally significant places of worship are college chapels. But while members of the university prayed in isolation, the town itself was accommodated in churches attached to each urban parish or indeed those which when the settlement was smaller fell in the surrounding villages. These latter buildings are for the most part unimposing medieval churches built of limestone but perhaps the most obvious exception to this rule is St Mary, Iffley. This is Norman Romanesque at its most unspoilt, the repeated patterns somehow amplified by its recent coats of homogenising limewash. The characteristic details: chevron, sawtooth and, most oddly of all, beakhead are what define this period before the more ambitious engineering of the middle and late medieval period. Vaults and ribs and ever more elaborate tracery dominate the building. There is something Norse and rough to us about the dramatic features of these bird creatures. They shout out the French conquerors' ancestry but the actual masons were English and of Anglo-Saxon descent, so perhaps they are just a last gasp of the 'dark ages' of illumination, dragons and general devilry. The tower of St Michael at the North Gate predates Iffley and is a survivor of Saxon Oxford with its bulbous balusters (extraordinarily they were turned on a lathe) and round topped arch.

The only really outstanding medieval church in Oxford is St Mary (the university church). With its soaring spire emerging from ranks of crocketed pinnacles it dominates the roofscape of central Oxford and it is well worth climbing the tower (and queueing for the chance to do so) as you get the best views of the town from there. For centuries the church was the place of assembly for the university as well as a place of worship. Other churches have fallen out of their original uses instead being fitted out as libraries. The college libraries of St Edmund Hall and Lincoln are satisfactory new uses for St Peter-in-the-East and All Saints respectively, both externally unchanged but inside transformed. Further from the centre, parishes that were once outlying or even rural have been folded into the city; St Giles and St Thomas the Martyr are part of central Oxford while village churches like Headington, Wolvercote and Hinksey have become suburban. The expansion of Oxford's suburbs in the nineteenth century called for new places of worship. The gauntly Grecian St Paul, Walton Street (currently serving whisky sours as Freud's bar rather than Eucharistic wine) is a landmark that seems to have almost completely lost its ecclesiastical character.

In stark contrast nearby St Barnabas is a beacon of the lasting influence of the Oxford Movement in worship. The church's Italianate tower with its shallow slopes and its copper cap looms behind any view of Jericho and its long terraces of artisan cottages, whose inhabitants formed St Barnabas's original congregation. More romantically it can be seen from across the open space of Port Meadow, looking to the comparatively minded like the cathedral of Torcello in the Venetian lagoon. This misty fantasy has been slightly dented by the completion of a graceless set of university accommodation blocks that skirt the railway line. The cause of much discontent and correspondence, these buildings are at best a careless expression of high handed bad manners and they stand in Oxford as a rare example of poorly executed commercial architecture in a visually important setting.

Back across the canal and entering the unassuming south door of St Barnabas the extent of the influence of Northern Italy becomes apparent. A basilica with apse, clerestory and bold Byzantine columns is lavishly decorated in various degrees of finish. The glass mosaics are incomplete but the low stone screen (in provenance straight from Torcello) and the stencilled and almost stage-painterly effect of the apse of 1869 combined with an elaborate painted pulpit of 1890 produce a memorable interior. The space is all the more dramatic because it is in such stark contrast to the dour rendered exterior elevations.

Pevsner's description of every town and village in the country begins and focuses on the churches of that place. They receive what for many readers might seem a disproportionate degree of attention but, for the first half millennium of surviving British architecture, ecclesiastical building was the principal focus of resources. The discrepancy between buildings constructed for religious use and the mass of lower status domestic and commercial structures was stark. Often the only stone building in a settlement, or in larger and more established towns of cut stone, was the church. Churches became and remained the visually dominant elements in most English landscapes, as emphasised by their towers or spires depending on the region. This idea survived the Reformation, as did most parish churches, and while increasing development may have diluted their prominence, the ecclesiological movement and religious revival of the mid nineteenth century meant that again the church was the most significant and carefully designed building in town. Oxford is, however, the exception to this rule. Most college buildings dwarf most churches and, with the signal exceptions of St Mary's and All Saints (now Lincoln College library), the dreaming spires of post-Reformation Oxford are dominated by collegiate building. Likewise much of what is most exciting is secular or, at any rate, intended primarily for educational use. This is not just an architectural observation for the parish church is essentially a public space, the property of the whole community while a college hall, library or chapel is specifically restricted to use by members of the college. Oxford's best buildings are essentially private although the public are invited to view them at pre-ordained times. All of this makes the parish churches of Oxford a side show and not the principal act in this dramatic and extravagant architectural circus.

St CROSS church c 1160. Tower (late 13) In the churchyard
is buried the Author Kenneth Graham, writer of 'Wind in The
Willows'. This Village church is no longer in use for worship
and has become Balliol college library extension

St Ebbe's church is hidden in the edge of the loathesome
Westgate centre - The principal survivor of "improvements"
that all but wiped out this part of the medieval city. Given
Abbey of Eynsham in 1141 - west door (shown here) is 1170
decorated with Zig-Zag and beakhead. Tower mainly rebuilt
by G.E. Street in 1862-66. 2 Good windows with Plate tracery

DETAIL of DECORATED RIBS in Church of St PETER in the EAST. Chains representing Chains of St Peter c. 1160.

DETAIL of BEAK-HEAD CARVING in St MARY, IFFLEY... 1170s. The church has first class Norman carving

Tower of St Giles' church. Twin light
Bell - opening in early C13 top storey

CARFAX Tower, all that remains of a C14
church of St Martin. That was rebuilt
as a Regency Gothic model ITSELF to
be demolished in a road widening
project of 1896. Tower re-faced by
T·G·Jackson (so prolific he was known as
'OXFORD JACKSON')

St Michael at The Northgate c 1000 - 1050. This is
on the site of the Old North Gate in the now-
demolished town wall. This is BOLD, TOUGH
building so perhaps why it has lasted 1000
years. ALSO This saxon church is made
of hard un-carvable local RAGSTONE which
has resisted The centuries of wear and
Tear

These alternate legnth QUOINS
are a saxon feature called
LONG & SHORT WORK......

St Andrew's Headington. (13 Tower with Norman church later
rebuilt. 1862 J.C. Buckler nave and further work in 1880.
This church forms part of a very rural composition;
fine church house and picturesque cottages some of them
thatched make clear how Oxford has grown to envelop a
number of pretty villages in sub-standard (20 suburbia...

Across the meadows from West Oxford and the
flooding of Osney is SOUTH HINKSEY and the
Church of St LAURENCE. A simple and unassuming
church of local ragstone. Chunk C13 with early
georgian chancel.

PORCH of 1621. St Thomas The
Martyr, tucked away in a church-
-yard full of Bee-hives and drug
dealers, has a remarkable interior
with a wholeheartedly eclectic
collection of ecclesiastical items
scatted THICKLY about. Italian
Gilt candlesticks and paintings
Painted beams and stations of
the cross... smells nicely of incense

St Thomas was founded in 1142 by
now invisible OSNEY ABBEY. Tower
is perpendicular but much else
re-built or restored

COWLEY Rd Methodist Church. 1903 by Stephen
Salter 1826-96 A good example of the free-ranging,
un-fettered and imaginative fantasy of the late
Gothic revival ALTHOUGH to Label it thus would
be... restrictive. It is as much an essay in
asymmetrical baroque as in new-look perpendicular
Easy to walk past but worth looking at as is the
dismissive description in Pevsner...

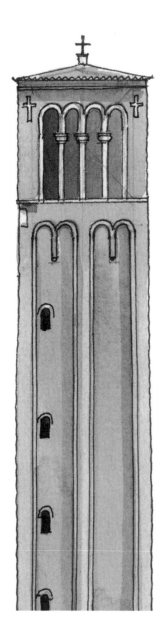
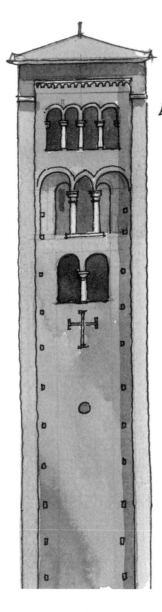

this shallow HAT of 1892 replaced a steeper original

These bells called mourners to DANTE's Funeral in 1321

Church was built, arcades, apse, all profoundly ITALIAN in 1887

Two towers to compare. on the left S. Maria Assunta in Torcello (Romantic horizon-piercing tower in the Venetian Lagoon) & on the Right, S. Francesco in Ravenna BOTH are good examples of the BYZANTINE school of this so called DARK AGES.....

...That inspired the design of St BARNABAS. "strength, solidity & thoroughly sound construction" were stipulations of the founder Thomas Combe (Superintendent of the Clarendon press). He continued "not a penny is to be thrown away on external appearance and decoration"... The Architect Arthur Blomfield satisfied these demands

St Mary. The Parish church of Oxford called 'the University Church as for Centuries the University was governed from this building. It is the ultimate DREAMING SPIRE. Tower is of c 1290-1320 and spire restored Gilbert Scott in 1856 · Extra ORDINARY porch is covered in Baroque chapter but really the fantastic Crocketted pinnacles are fairly Baroque themselves. The CONGREGATION house (used until 1488) has fine Vaults c1320-1330.

St Mary Iffley. NORMAN MASTERPIECE c1170-80, one of the best preserved C13 churches in ENGLAND. C19 restoration included bringing roofline back to its original pitch and introduced The frieze and small window at The top. Rich and elaborate decoration and now BOLD limewash makes it worth the slog (hot by foot) up the Iffley Rd

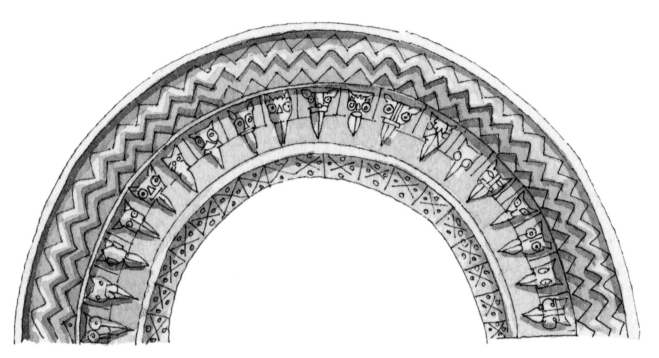

Re-set S. DOORWAY. St Peter in the east with
bulbous Chevron and Beak heads c. 1160s

St Margaret. BINSEY set a PICTURESQUE Walk across Port
Meadow. Doorway late C13. good Eric Gill carving on Pulpit

PISCINA (13 in Binsey Church

Holy Well, the model for the Treacle well in Alice in Wonderland. It was caused to produce healing waters by the prayers of St Frideswide and became a place of Pilgrimage

St Philip & St James (Phil & Jim) built 1862 by G.E. Street to accommodate worshippers in the newly established suburb of N. Oxford. Steeple of 1866

St Paul. Walton St
1836 H.J. Underwood
GRECIAN ELEGANCE
now sells Cocktails
instead...

EVD

St ALBAN. Charles St off COWLEY Rd ~ barely mentioned by Persner (only that it contains E. Gill Stations of the cross.) Built in 1928-1933 by T.L. Dale. Not dramatic but with a graceful repeating arcade of DIOCLETIAN Windows.

Iffley Old Rectory. There has been a church house here for almost as long as the church. The current building Pre-dates-, in part, the reformation. It was described in 1475 as "The house wherein the Parish Priest hath been used to dwell."

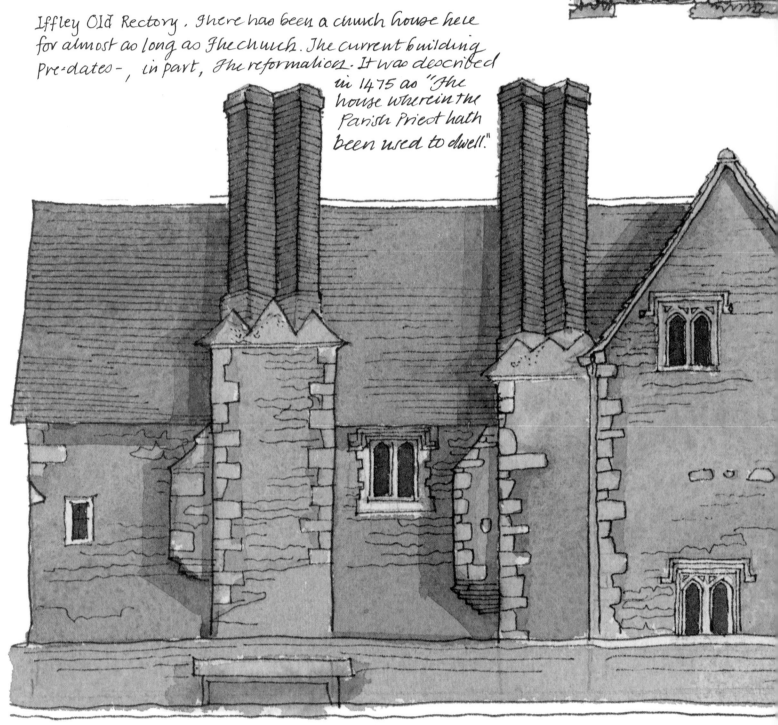

Nicolas Stone 1586/7 - 1647 built the South Porch of St Mary in 1637: Solomonic (Barleysugar) Columns, volutes and a wildly baroque explosive pediment are <u>unmatched</u> in the country

REFORMATION
AND RESTORATION

1536–1700

The dissolution of the monasteries changed Britain's whole economic system. Henry VIII's appropriation of the church's bulging property portfolio swelled both his own royal coffers and spread capital further into the pockets of the 'new men' who, benefitting from this glut of ex-ecclesiastical property, quickly formed a cadre of wealthy lawyers, local gentry and financial adventurers, some of whom would in due course endow the university with new gifts and establish new colleges: St John's College and Trinity College were both founded in this way in 1555. But first the tidal wave of the Reformation closed most colleges and wiped away the great friaries to the west of Oxford and the abbeys of Rewley and Osney. St Frideswide's survived the onslaught as part of the new Christ Church. This institution, established with the energetic support of the King was the most treasured project of his secretary Cardinal Wolsey. It was established as Cardinal College with the assistance of his successor as courtier Thomas Cromwell who was quickly afterwards found working to dismantle the foundation and re-establish it as Christ Church, incorporating the abbey church of St Frideswide (she was a local Saxon saint) into the new institution. The original project was interrupted mid-way by Wolsey's dramatic fall from grace, and this moment is set in stone, manifested by the corbels built to support the vault of a huge cloister in Tom Quad which was never to be constructed. Meanwhile here, as everywhere else in the country, abbey churches and complexes were either demolished (and the materials then sometimes reused in the building of secular mansions for the 'new men'), or they were simply employed as easy quarries of cut stone. This was logical standard practice when castles or barns fell out of use,

although there was a degree of unease among the principled when the sacred stones of a well-loved church were carted away. These qualms were, however, quickly side stepped and while some of the great monastic ruins, particularly in the more remote parts of the country, survived as the focus of antiquarian and romantic interest, the great religious houses of Oxford disappeared almost without trace leaving only a drab fragment of a door set deep in a supermarket, or a window frame in a roadside wall. The Carmelite foundation of Gloucester College, established to train clerks for a number of monastic establishments was re-founded as Gloucester Hall in 1541, and survived in fragile form until its new life began as Worcester College in 1714.

While the college system had been in place for three hundred years by the Reformation many undergraduate students lived in independent halls. These were run by an individual master ('magister') who organised accommodation (a bed and a place to study) and a dining hall. These were later either to be incorporated into existing colleges, until then the preserve of graduates, or to become colleges themselves. These changes in the university and indeed in the (employing) church itself resulted in smaller numbers than ever before of students enrolling in the university. The newly established Church of England required priests and curates and indeed church lawyers so the university, even in its reduced state, survived the tidal wave. Just as church building was all but abandoned in this time (after a final flourish of perpendicular Gothic extravagance under the last two Henries) so the university was correspondingly becalmed. It was not until the beginning of the seventeenth century that serious new building began and also the establishment of new colleges. With this renaissance of university activity came the first whisperings of a new style as the architectural language of ancient Rome as interpreted by fifteenth- and sixteenth-century Italy made its way north. Initially this was in the form of pattern books mainly printed in the Netherlands. These were of inestimable importance and they promulgated the new style. Columns and classical capitals replaced shafts and Gothic caps, balustrades in place of crenellations and cornices for cresting. Arched windows that looked back to early modern Britain gave way to classical surrounds that framed the view of far off Italy. And, once digested, this new information was quickly expressed in limestone. But change in preference is gradual and the Jacobean period is characterised by the initial introduction of classical elements; for example, the tower of the orders at the Bodleian (p 73) with the persistent survival of the Gothic in the labelling of the surrounding elevations (p 72). In this case two discrete architectural schools of thought sit uneasily side by side. Nearby in the chapel of Brasenose College (p 67) the two styles are combined in a single element, a swooping Gothic-Renaissance confection of a window that waves forward and back, as it looks south to the university church, all crockets and finials, and east to the Palladian correctness of the Radcliffe Camera. Canterbury Quad in St John's College (1635) is a proper Italian cloister with repeating round arches and classical columns in place of the cusped and pointed Gothic of Magdalen. The Renaissance was by now confidently taking root in Oxford and the path was made clear for the rule of classicism that, in various forms, would last for two centuries.

As mentioned in the introduction (p 7) Oxford took on the mantle of royal power in 1642 when Charles I was obliged to move the Stuart court from London in order to avoid the parliamentarians. The architectural sophistication of Oxford and its collegiate nature meant it was fairly well suited to its role as a temporary seat of government. Other towns within reach of the capital would have had a town or a guild hall and several large churches (or even a castle), but none offered a comparably powerful collection of potential meeting places, let alone similarly comfortable accommodation. The Reformation had also changed the status of heads of house from celibate to potentially married. As well as effecting a social change in the university and producing an opportunity for some good high-status domestic building, this also provided enhanced accommodation during the Oxford parliament.

While the Interregnum was no more productive architecturally in Oxford than in the rest of the country the Restoration of Charles II marked a new vigour in development and meanwhile the faltering language of classicism gained fluency and confidence and the last remnants of Gothic were all but cast aside. Christopher

Wren's Sheldonian Theatre of 1669 was a powerful statement of historicism both in its superficial dress (here it is Roman), but also in its function. It is a re-imagining of a building of the ancients pressed into service for modern Oxford. It forms part of what is perhaps the most outstandingly beautiful collection of variegated buildings in the country rather like those of the Piazza San Marco in Venice or the centre of Mantua. It is interesting in its own right as Wren's first great work, but it also set the tone for the next phase of Oxford's building. Across the paved yard is the Clarendon building. Again, it is a bold statement in the new mode. Two massive temple fronts, the columns semi-attached and powerful, sandwiching a rectangular box seeming to squeeze it upwards. Although the building is long, its effect is vertical and entirely due to its soaring tree trunk columns. The architect is Nicholas Hawksmoor (1715) who also worked at All Souls. With Vanbrugh building the grandest house in Britain, Blenheim Palace, nearby, the three great English baroque architects were together defining the new architecture in Oxford.

FELLOWS' QUAD. Merton College: The first 3 storey
College in Oxford 1610 Simpler 4 tier
FRONTISPIECE than BODLEIAN.

JESUS College chapel consecrated 1621.
Gothic and Classical sitting alongside
one another. Porch of 1700

Oriel College. Front Quad. East Range 1637~42
Hall. Porch was rebuilt 1897. Stone Lettering reads
REGNANTE CAROLO. Above 2 statues of Edward II
& Charles The Martyr. BVM above. Remarkable
for its date is The classical Pediment at the top
(ie. not Jacobean cresting)

CHRIST CHURCH. HALL. c 1529 : Uffenbach writes in 1710 that it
is "fearfully large & high but otherwise poor & ugly in appear-
-ance.. It also reeks so STRONGLY of BREAD & MEAT that one cannot
remain in it. I should find it impossible to dine or live there."
In FACT it is splendid with Hammerbeam roof and the largest
pre-Victorian hall in either Oxford or Cambridge.

"All Souls is to be rebuilt QUITE NEW and in UNIQVE style
as SOON as POSSIBLE"... more from UFFENBACH in 1710. He was
Correctly informed... Nicholas Hawksmoor c 1661~1736 was
asked to provide designs for this and favoured Gothic over Classical
he (N.H.) wrote in 1715 advising the college to preserve "Antient
durable publick buildings... instead of erecting new, fantasticall, perishable TRASH"

This gatehouse is the
middle of THE WEST
Range & is completed
in 1734

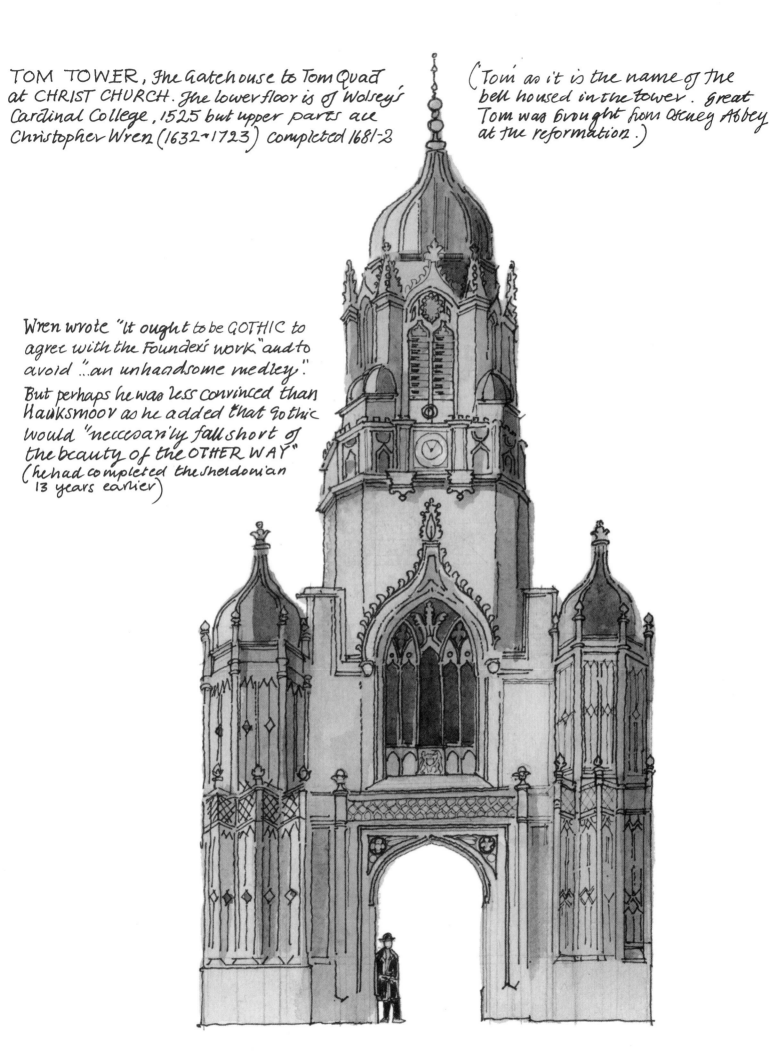

TOM TOWER, the Gatehouse to Tom Quad at CHRIST CHURCH. The lower floor is of Wolsey's Cardinal College, 1525 but upper parts are Christopher Wren (1632-1723) completed 1681-2

(Tom as it is the name of the bell housed in the tower. Great Tom was brought from Osney Abbey at the reformation.)

Wren wrote "It ought to be GOTHIC to agree with the Founder's work" and to avoid "...an unhandsome medley".
But perhaps he was less convinced than Hawksmoor as he added that Gothic would "neccesarily fall short of the beauty of the OTHER WAY" (he had completed the Sheldonian 13 years earlier)

The Sheldonian Theatre, Christopher Wren (1632-1723)
His first building in Oxford as well as his first ever DESIGN
Based on Serlio's drawing of the theatre of Marcellus in Rome
The FIRST CLASSICAL BUILDING in OXFORD.

LANTERN
is by BLORE · 1787-1879
and of 1837.

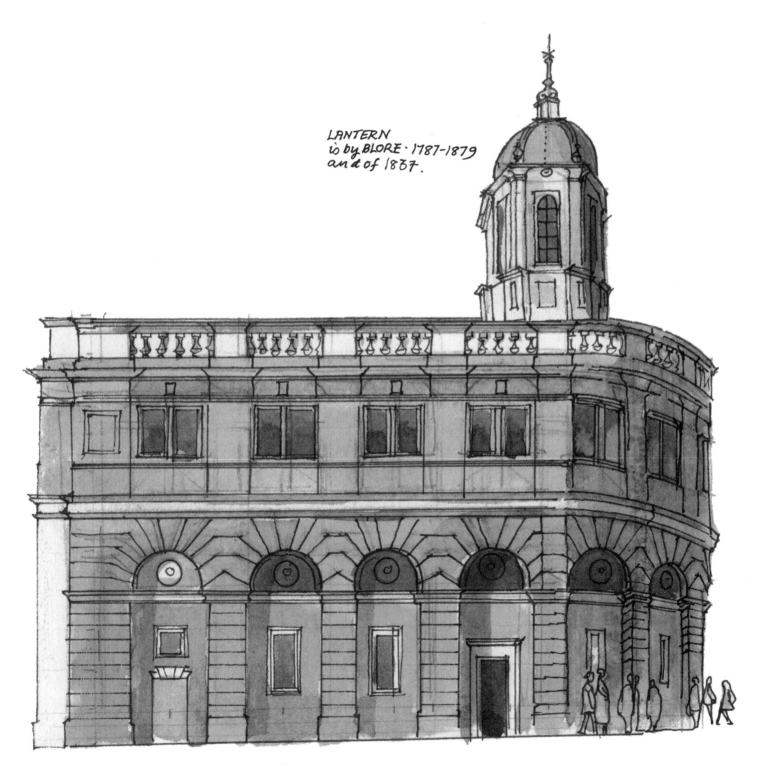

USING Palladio's double temple-front Motif
Wren makes a singular but dignified
facade. Pevsner is a fearful old PRIG about
every deviation from some imagined norm
but it is strong and remarkable....

... The Sheldonian again ....

The Sculptor Michael Black (d 2019) carved these heads The original "Ragged regiment" had all but decomposed in 1972...

REFORMATION AND RESTORATION

BRASENOSE CHAPEL · 1656 · 1666 an extraordinary
fusion of BAROQUE and GOTHIC · No Architect is known
but the Mason is John Jackson who was also Chief
mason on Canterbury Quad in St JOHNS Coll.

PEMBROKE College CHAPEL 1732 · William Townsend · Wildly elaborate
INTERIOR of 1884 in the ENGLISH RENNAISANCE STYLE (worth seeing...)

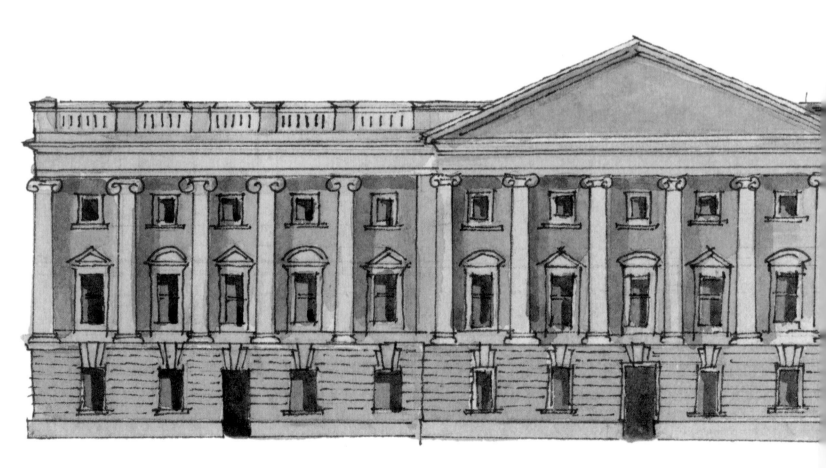

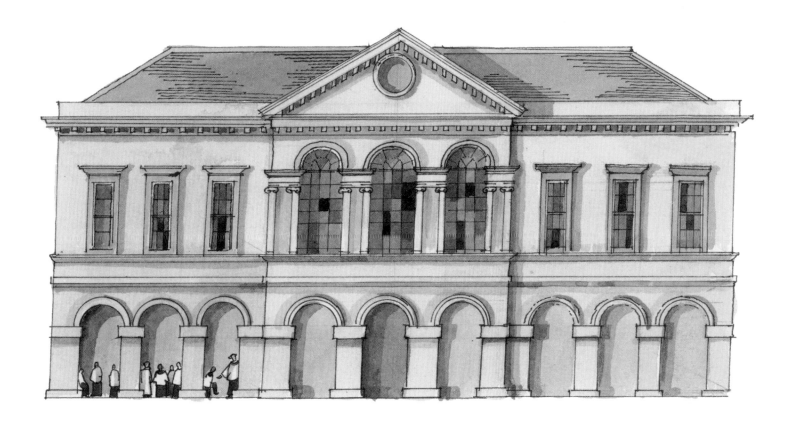

WORCESTER Coll. CHAPEL, LIBRARY & HALL .. Geo. CLARKE 1661 - 1736 . . WEST FACADE 1736. Dr CLARKE
CONSULTED HAWKSMOOR

CHRIST CHURCH. PECKWATER QUAD ·1705-14
HENRY ALDRICH 1647 ~ 1710 · ALDRICH was Dean
of CHRISTCHURCH , Scholar , Musician , Composer
and Architect ··· a POLYMATH

Anthony Wood 1632~1695 was at MERTON in 1652 after graduating he remained in OXFORD adding a letter to his name Anthony A'Wood. He is the father of ANTIQUARIANISM and despite never again being PART of the University (he was AWKWARD) but from 1660 when he gained access to its Archive he worked on the study of Oxfords Antiquities.

Wood desired to "advance" his "esurient genie in antiquities" despite his unconventional use of language and prickly personality his work on the City and the County of Oxfordshire is the most powerful view into the ⑰

This carving is STRAP WORK and is a peculiarity of the end of the ⑯ and early ⑰. It is in part derived from early Classical Pattern books but is still, despite curls and volutes an expression of the GOTHIC rather than the NEW.. Classical

All Souls Coll. East side of N Quad
2 Hawksmoor Gothic towers like
his work at WESTMINSTER ABBEY
c1734

71

Detail of Door

TOWER of the ORDERS SCHOOLS QUADRANGLE
This conceit. That a gatehouse should illustrate
the grammar of Classical orders IN ORDER. There
are five orders: Tuscan, Doric, Ionic, Corinthian
& on the top COMPOSITE. Similar but LESSER
versions of these can be seen at Burghley, Hatfield
& formerly at Somerset House. Despite the language
being Classical the windows remain gothic
and it is topped with CRESTING. STRAPWORK
& GOTHIC PINNACLES. a FANFARE for the end of
the Middle Ages

DIVINITY SCHOOLS. The PROSCHOLIUM - a grand hall, a narthex, built 1612. No named Architect but Masons ACKROYD, & BENTLEY (s): The ULTIMATE PERPENDICULAR BUILDING even though Stone's gate to the BOTANIC GARDEN was only 18 years away..

Magdalen College · CLOISTER 1475-90

St John's College · CANTERBURY QUAD 1611 - 1621 ~ 1636

Nicolas Stone 1632/3 - One of three Gateways
to the Botanic Gardens. VERMICULATED (worm eaten)
rustication. and a thorough exploration
of the Ancient Roman gatehouse
as recorded by SERLIO.
RICHER and far more
EXTRAVAGANTLY carved
than the more reserved
work of Inigo Jones
OXFORD'S first classical
STRUCTURE is in fact
MANNERIST/BAROQUE

STONE was JONES' master mason at the
Banquetting house at whitehall - this is
more resonate of MASQUE than PALADIAN
BUILDINGS

BUILT to house some of Arundel Marbles

• SCREEN BETWEEN OLD ASHMOLEAN & DIVINITY
SCHOOLS

HOTELS, PUBS AND PAVILIONS

Oxford has had a tourist industry for almost eight hundred years. The focus has always been the university which has attracted visitors from around the world, but now the town itself draws nearly nine million visitors a year to look at the remarkable buildings. One million of those visitors choose to stay the night. In the winter anxious parents can be spotted slogging through nervous breakfasts with children in various degrees of swottishness awaiting interviews either for the university or more likely, if chaperoned, for the schools which sprung up in the city in the nineteenth century. There are several hotels for these gloomy rites of passage.

Oxford has a good ancient pub in the Mitre and there are other notable examples, but it is not a city of coaching inns. The traveller Zacharias Conrad von Uffenbach (1683-1734) wrote an account of his protracted visit of 1710. He had a fairly hard line on what was already a well established tradition of non-academic visiting to Oxford, stating that tourists 'gaze at the library as a cow might gaze at a new gate'. All these gawpers needed sustenance. Famously, Norwich was known to have a church for every week of the year and a pub for every day; perhaps in the great days of the public house Oxford had as many but there are still over a hundred pubs to slake the thirst of frayed physicists or exultant philosophers on the lam. Some have untouchable pedigrees of academic excellence having quietly emptied the great brains of centuries; others are celebrated for their location. Some are little different from the houses on either side, being just what their name implies: the same but public. These can be defined as such by a colour wash and modest signage. The Rose and Crown on North Parade offers a particularly fine example of this domestic typology.

In an age when so many pubs are being returned to private use Oxford is able to buck the trend, not least because most drinkers can stride out from their libraries, the terraces of Jericho or the Iffley and Cowley roads before stumbling back home without recourse to the car, thus avoiding the existential damage done to rural pubs by legal alcohol limits. The riverine character of the city and the tradition of punting as a means of romantic conquest, or as evidence of manly prowess, has made institutions of the Trout and the Perch, which sit in picturesque rural charm along the Thames and (for those weary punters) the Victoria Arms has gardens running down to the reedy banks of the river Cherwell. The pubs of literary reputation, such as the Eagle and Child in which J.R.R. Tolkien dreamt up his mystical Saxon fantasies, would be considered unexceptional in any other Midlands town, but here they are suffused with almost numinous mystique.

In 1864, twenty years after the arrival of the railway in Oxford, the Randolph Hotel opened. It remains the one great Victorian monument in Oxford to middle class travel. This monolithic giant was designed by William Wilkinson (1819-1901), who was to be one of the principal architects of the North Oxford suburbs. In terms of Victorian brilliance and ebullience the Randolph is underwhelming: practicality and pure scale do not make up for its under-articulated plainness, and its propinquity to the hugely imaginative Ashmolean/Taylorian composition over the road does not serve it well. But inside a series of impressive huge rooms and a remarkable series of paintings by Osbert Lancaster (1908-1986) make the tea rooms worth the visit. Two more hotels have caused other buildings to be repurposed.

The Old Parsonage is self-explanatory, although having tea in front of its fire (once roaring; now lamely flickering in gaseous parody) allows visitors to envy the former vicars of adjacent St Giles. Conversely the Old Bank in the High Street allows you to drink gin and tonics, or whisper sweet nothings, in rooms where indigent undergraduates once faced their bank managers, either in the wing collars of Victorian rectitude or the shiny suits and ties of the 1990s. Both buildings have been preserved by their reuse and remain lively players in their respective streetscapes.

Restaurants are not a historical building type in Oxford (despite the Grand Café being on the site of the first coffee house in Britain, which opened in 1650 according to the antiquary Anthony Wood) but, again, there are several interestingly converted buildings. A particularly striking example is the Central Boys' School (Leonard Stokes, 1901), a stylish Arts and Crafts building currently deliciously reborn as My Sichuan. It is architecturally distinguished with exaggerated detailing straying into the realms of art nouveau, but even more exciting is the stained glass inside. A series of faultless roundels, created to delight the boys who once attended the school, are now a good diversion from the chilli heaped treats that emerge from the kitchen which formerly dolloped out meat in gravy and rice pudding.

The university, and indeed Oxford's schools, celebrated the nineteenth-century obsession with physical fitness with a series of first rate sporting pavilions. The cricket pavilion is a good representative type. Verandaed and unpretentious, it has an almost irresistible fate to be picturesque. Even the version at St Edward's, designed in a pared down European international style (John Pawson, 2010), is a fine decoration for the lavish playing fields of that school. Boathouses, however, have been dealt a stingy hand in Oxford. Gloomy commercial functionalism has generally given them an undeserved pall of architectural gloom. Other examples along the Thames, in Twickenham or Putney for instance, developed a joyous vernacular of a New England type with fretted balconies and verandas. Only the Cherwell Boathouse, once again now repurposed as a successful restaurant, shows that this has, at least in the twentieth century, been an opportunity missed.

HOTELS, PUBS AND PAVILIONS

The Randolph Hotel was
built in 1863-6. Designed
by William Wilkinson (1819-
-1901) who was the first
main architect of N. Oxford.
Heavy handed and lacking
in character it is somehow
overscaled and never as
grand as its size demands.
... under-articulated it
needed more ... ideas ...

The Old Bank Hotel was the Oxford branch of Barclays Bank from 1775–1998 a good Georgian building it has swopped afternoon tea for overdrafts and martinis for mortgages...

The Old Parsonage, Banbury Rd. has a long
history and though it did have clerical
beginnings it has been let to series of tenants
for centuries. Nevertheless the fantasy that
it might have done service as the vicarage
still pervades the now velvetty interior.
The building is C17 and marks the top of
St Giles. A doorway carries the date 1659

curious fireplace which now burns with a
weedy gas flame

The Radcliffe Camera : James Gibbs 1682-1754
completed 1749. The bequest of Dr Radcliffe
who left £40,000 to build a library was made
before his death in 1714. He also funded
the observatory and J. Radcliffe hospital.

The Turl Tavern, a pub, frequently rather lowly since
1381 for much of that time called the spotted cow. It
being in Oxford rather than famous prize fighters
and window cleaners it has been the haunt of
youthful Presidents & Prime ministers

The Rose & Crown in North Parade, a pub since 1863, a small and domestic Bar. The antithesis to the huge commercial drinking house, has been of near mystic significance to students for nearly two centuries

The trout is a riverside country pub that has found itself in Oxford even though protected by the green fastness of port meadow...

Two more OXFORD PUBS - The Victoria built to cater for College servants and Artisans who settled in mid C19 Jericho. The Magdalen has a famous kitchen..

Combe house school behind St Thomas
The martyr (1702). Nobody changed the
Mullioned windows for sashes and
with heavy Plait Band and cornice
it looks earlier.

G.E. Street's (Qld) St Barnabas school in Clarendon St in Jericho is typically Austere and v. slightly under fenestrated. Heavy plate tracery & generous gables. A Tough School building for a robust suburb but still a stylish & remarkable building all the same and serious GOTHIC of 1855-1856 (was originally the St Paul's Industrial School)

LEONARD STOKES was asked to design three schools in 1901. The boys central school in Gloucester green is an arts and Crafts leaning building under a heavy stone slate roof. Inside (easy to see if you like Chinese food) the classrooms are built around a hall lit by a glazed dome with first rate painted glass panels. .... mannered.

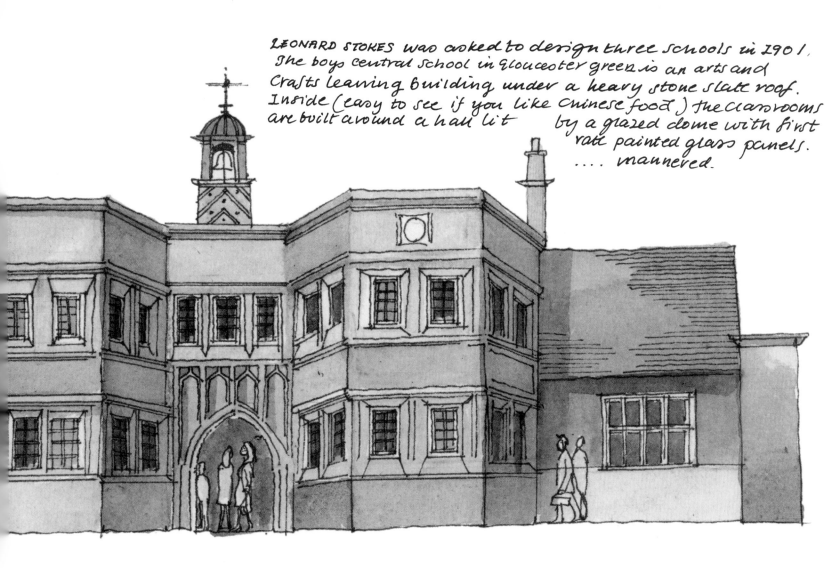

SPORTS PAVILION · QUEEN'S COLLEGE · Generous. Oak and a Sweeping hipped roof, a Heavy post and lintel Veranda and the College Arms. Playing fields by the river below Christ Church meadow. Edwardian Relaxation.

EFFORTLESSLY DULL and UNLOVELY BOATHOUSES · OPPORTUNITY MISSED · · · ·

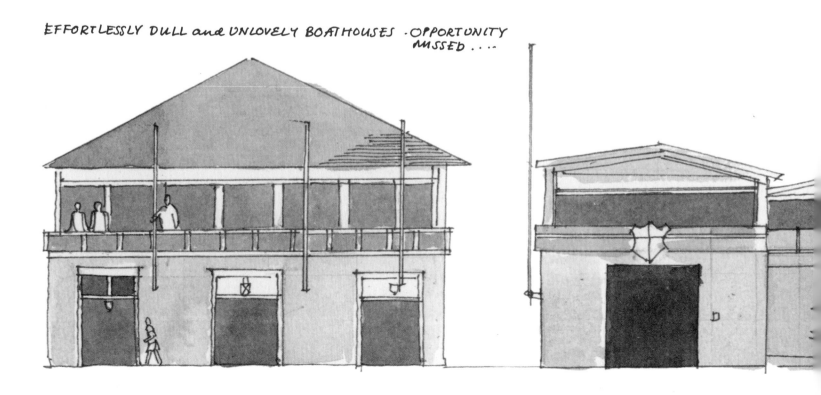

WORCESTER COLLEGE has lavish and verdant policies, Orchard and Glasshouses, borders and lawns and a picturesque lake with lazily overhanging trees. unusually the College playing fields are ... on site. and so their Pav' is unsurprisingly a decoration to the College

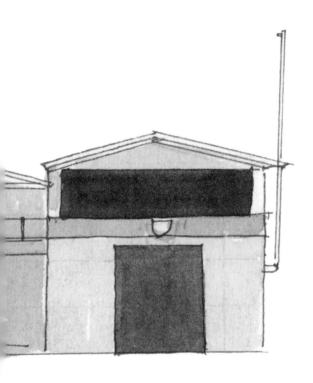

OXFORD has not ONE but TWO small Art-house cinemas where culture-chomping locals QUEUE politely and conversationally to see the latest mildly pornographic french film. Quietly commercial pictures are also shown. Essential Art Deco lines

the OLDEST cinema in town of 1910/11, saw news reels of the great war. a period piece...

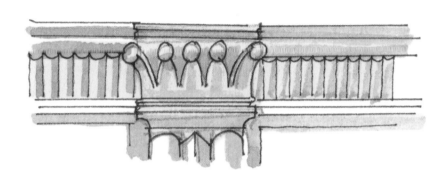

The former REGAL cinema in Cowley Rd was opened in 1937 and listed Grade 2 in 2004. As with its many contemporaries it escaped the wrecker's ball by posing grandly as a Bingo Hall and Night Club. now it is a Giant Church when tiny Parish Churches rattle emptily.. They must be doing something right. Built in the pared down Egyptian style that followed Howard Carter and Lord Caenarvon's discovery of the tomb of
TUTANKHAMUN...

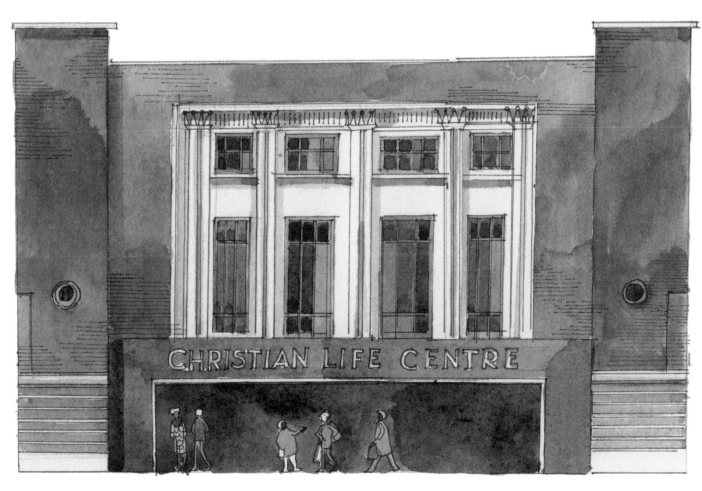

GEORGIAN OXFORD

1700–1830

The atmosphere of Oxford changed. In the increasingly secular and wealthy late seventeenth and eighteenth century the church atrophied and ecclesiastical buildings fell into disrepair and ruin. Pluralism was rife. This was the situation where one man could take the livings of several parishes, leaving an impecunious curate to maintain a desultory observance for an increasingly disinterested congregation. All parish income was diverted to the frequently distant cleric who was more concerned with the blood lines of hounds than the blood of Christ the Saviour. In this worldly atmosphere the university at Oxford changed its focus. Rather than the education of the astute and earnest it was that of the privileged and well-heeled that fuelled the architectural developments of the mid and late eighteenth century in Oxford. These strapping well-fed undergraduates emerging from Eton, Winchester and Harrow were well travelled and had grown up in the great houses of Britain. Not for them a monkish cell, a rude pallet or a simple desk and stool. They, or their parents, had higher standards and as they became the model student so the architecture of the university changed, unsubtly, to reflect their status. Any references to monasticism, or indeed medievalism, were cast aside until the end of the eighteenth century, and then only appeared in superficial detailing and outward clothing. Ranges of bold repeating classical temple fronts, arcades and colonnades lined the quads of colleges in sympathy, or even competition, with Britain's grandest country houses. Canterbury Quad at Christ Church, most of Queen's College and the new buildings at Magdalen (the last of these even situated in a deer park) all made the scions of the country's increasingly

wealthy and worldly aristocracy and gentry (known as commoners as opposed to scholars) find in the university a comfort and familiarity. This placed heavy demands on colleges who, searching for more sites on which to erect appropriately palatial accommodation for their students acquired their neighbours: smaller and less well funded Halls. The colleges either incorporated or merely demolished these Halls to make way for more grandiose projects.

As the eighteenth century hit its middle years the ebullient baroque expressions of the Stuarts and the house of Orange gave way to a more considered, restrained and less theatrical employment of architectural classicism. The breathless piling of architectural elements employed by Wren, Gibbs and Hawksmoor was abandoned; this was the end for their bold and convention-busting dreams. It was replaced by the more Palladian, austere and analytical classicism that epitomises the refined high Georgian period. This elegance and grandeur defined Oxford for eighty years and the city has many good examples of it. The later neo-classical Greek revival never really gets a look in with its bleak Doric order and footless columns. With the exception of one building, the Greek revival is largely absent from Oxford in this period.

The energy and enthusiasm with which the masters and fellows of the colleges adopted this change was tempered with a sensible innate conservatism and economy. In the world of the country house, inflamed by the passions of the grand tour, the returning Lord tore down the Tudor or Jacobean hall that had suited his grandfather so well and threw up in its place temples from Rome sitting brightly among the ancient oaks, thus utterly re-defining the generic idea of the gentleman's seat. But in the common rooms of Oxford decisions of a less thorough nature were taken and, while plenty of what went before was wiped away (frequently the domestic architecture of non-university medieval Oxford), the two opposing styles were juggled side by side. It is this series of dramatic contrasts, ameliorated only by the consistent use of one building material which provided a superficial but visually restful homogeneity, that characterises the Oxford that was the background for the nineteenth century and the architectural earthquake that accompanied it...

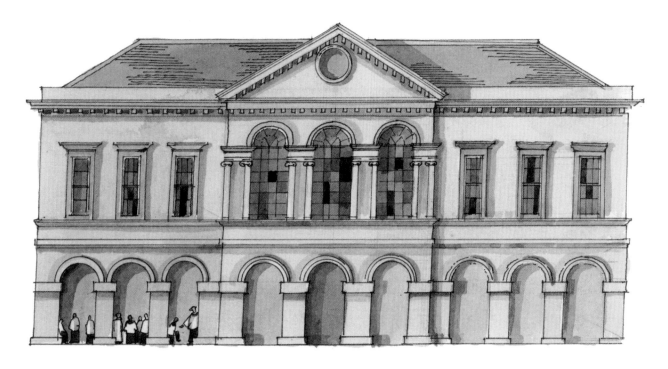

CORPUS CHRISTI *FELLOWS' BUILDING*
1706 ~ 1712 *Possibly by Dean Aldrich*
(1648·1710) Paladian .

NEW BUILDINGS MAGDALEN COLLEGE
1733 *prob by G. Clarke (1661·1736) Gibbs helps*
The Ultimate Country House college building it is even built in a Deer Park.
Uffenbach records "numerous white & spotted stags"

The CLARENDON building 1711-15. funded
by the profits of Earl of Clarendon's BEST SELLER
"The history of the great Rebellion" pub. 1702-4.
DESIGNED by Nicholas Hawksmoor c. 1661-1736
To house The UNIVERSITY PRESS

Bold English Baroque, GRANDIOSE & DRAMATIC
4 GIANT ORDER TUSCAN COLUMNS all set on a
heavy PLINTH. Above are lead statues of the
MUSES by Thornhill (1675-1734). DORIC FRIEZE
Completes the CLASSICAL TEMPLE FORM loved
by HAWKSMOOR. A ROMAN Temple of LEARNING

CORINTHIAN CAPITAL of Great Elegance in The
RADCLIFFE OBSERVATORY with finest carved
Acanthus scrolls . Henry KEENE designed
This in 1772 but it is completed by WYATT
(1746~1813) . EXTREME GEORGIAN ELEGANCE

PLASTER CEILING in QUEEN'S COLLEGE LIBRARY
JAMES HANDS · 1695

also .... ELEGANT FOLIAGE, PALMETTES & SCROLLS carved by
Thomas Roberts, 1756
No Longer BAROQUE but ROCOCO.

CHRIST CHURCH LIBRARY 1717-1722 ~ CLARKE (1661-1736)
At The time cost £15,000, Still Baroque with Giant Order
Corinthian Columns starting at the ground

Oriel Library 1788 (James Wyatt 1746-1813) on a
rusticated lower storey

LIBRARY at QUEEN'S COLLEGE 1692-5. Architect unknown perhaps ALDRICH. He was Dean of Christ Church and was Doyen of Oxford Architecture at the Time. Nods to WREN'S LIBRARY at TRINITY Coll Cambridge in that it is raised above in *This* case a rusticated lower story and in Cambridge a DORIC ARCADE

CORPUS CHRISTI College CLOISTER 1706-12 · Wm Townesend rebuilt in 1962

TRINITY COLLEGE GATES & PIERS 1713 Wm Townesend (1676~1739)
with Ironwork by Thomas Robinson

QUEEN'S COLLEGE . SCREEN
WEST RANGE 1709-11
RECESSED WINDOWS, a motif taken from Hugh May's
work at windsor of 1675

CHRIST CHURCH Canterbury Quad Gate 1773-83
James Wyatt 1746-1814 . Powerful late georgian
in TRIUMPHAL ARCH Mode.
One Arch, 8 Blank niches . . .

GEORGIAN OXFORD

St Edmund Hall. East Range. Library Above. c. 1680 no known Architect
The PEDIMENT on the door rests on a FRIEZE BOOK-ENDED with PILES of BOOKS

O.U.P Central three bays 1826-30
Daniel Robertson. Latest CLASSICAL
in TRIUMPHAL ARCH FORM

GEORGIAN OXFORD

RADCLIFFE OBSERVATORY begun 1772 Henry Keene (1726 - 1776) and completed 1794 · James Wyatt (1746 - 1813) Pevsner says "The architecturally finest Observatory of Europe". Model in The TOWER of The WINDS · ATHENS

QUEEN'S COLLEGE · GATEHOUSE 1734
Architect unknown · Banded vermiculated
columns and fine rustication · Above an open
Topped ROTUNDA · Statue of Queen Caroline
wife of GEORGE II

ALL SAINTS Church NOW LINCOLN COLLEGE
Library.. 1706-1708 poss Dean Aldrich poss
Peshall. A fine London City church Landed
in OXFORD. Steeple modified after consultation
with HAWKSMOOR

BRASENOSE

TRINITY

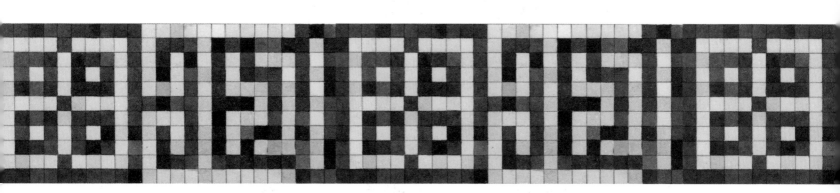

Three decorative black & white marble floors

STREETS AND HOUSES

The two great streets of Oxford, the High Street and Broad Street, are among the most celebrated linear architectural compositions in the country. Whether they unfold to the guidebook toting foot-tourist or greet the bleary eye of the reveller returning to Oxford on the midnight bus, they have as components such a remarkable richness of facades and such an articulation of towers, domes, pinnacles and crenellations that it is hard to think of a more serious contender for best English street in terms of architecture. But while they are studded with temple fronts and turrets, the setting is one of straightforward colour washed frontages for medieval town houses. Some are hidden behind rendered faux stone facades; others like 26-27 Cornmarket have had their polite Georgian masks carefully peeled away to reveal timber studded structures of the fifteenth century with jettied upper storeys that so characterise houses and shops of this date all over the country. Drawings of Oxford before the great Victorian spate of expansion and rebuilding show many more temptingly lavish and highly decorated gabled buildings of this type which would have made the middle of town feel slightly more like other great Midlands towns and cities. The collegiate and university building spree gave Oxford its extraordinary character but at the cost of much picturesque vernacular building. Second to these great set pieces is St Giles, the broad road the heads north before splitting at its eponymous church. Here elegant Georgian houses line the road. Most impressive is St Giles House of 1702 built by Bartholomew Peisley who also built Vanbrugh House in St Michael's Street, the Hall and Library at St Edmund Hall and Stone's Almshouses on St Clement's Street.

It is a remarkable aspect of the late seventeenth and eighteenth century that as well as the great output of Britain's important baroque and classical architects (Vanbrugh, Hawksmoor, Wren, and, later, Kent, Adam, Wyatt, Cockerell and Soane) there sprung up a cadre of very much less well known practitioners, barely defined as architects as opposed to builders. These men worked not as students or vapid copiers but as co-travellers. They also read, saw and digested the great books and buildings, knew Vitruvius and Palladio (Inigo Jones's copy of Palladio is in the Worcester College library) and visited Paris and Rome. They understood, even if not they did not actually lead, the great project of classical architecture. The less distinguished practitioners – builders and developers who would not have considered themselves architects – still wielded pediments and cornices with general confidence and understanding in a way that has now become the private and more esoteric passion of a rather more select club of practitioners. This passing on of knowledge with minimal dilution of clarity continued when the Corinthian and the Ionic slept like mid morning party-goers in irrelevant and unfashionable shame and while, with new minted assumed moral authority, the cusp and the crocket ruled the Victorian Gothic roost.

While the centre of Oxford is a remarkable set piece of survival (and revival) allowing the very least of ill mannered intrusions from the age of modernism, the outer fringes are a contrast to this grandeur. Beaumont Street, one of two pieces of standard issue Georgian town planning, is a fine set of wings to the backcloth of Worcester College but it is a street that could just as easily be in Cheltenham or Warwick, let alone Bath or Bristol. South of the centre the

medieval quarter of St Ebbe's was wiped away in the 1960s to shrieks of antiquarian distress and all to enable the erecting of the unlamented Westgate shopping centre. This witless and gloomy street-denying development has now itself been crushed to landfill and a childishly breathless brave new retail world has replaced it in contemporary clothes. This humourless leviathan is less offensive that its predecessor but could so easily have squatted down on the edge of town, perhaps rejuvenating the Temple Cowley area, leaving this significant plot free for much needed housing and university development. Developers and planners seemed unable to make the leap, or to recognise that encouraging out-of-town shoppers to brave the choking bottlenecks of Abingdon and Cowley roads only to enter an air conditioned shopping mall might be futile. They could not see that shopping and vital retail jobs might have been happily housed in an area with suitable transport and service networks. In other towns and cities the out-of-town move can do inestimable damage to the economy of a city centre by leaving a bleak 'donut', but here the power of the university would clearly have stopped this from occurring.

Beyond are the tidy terraces of Jericho, which in their way are as remarkable a survival as the great sweeps of historic Oxford. Repeated plans to sweep away this artisan suburb were curbed and now the tiny cottages which were designed to house the builders, railwaymen and foundry workers of Victorian Oxford (as well as the more picturesque project of housing the printers of the Oxford University Press) are safe. No longer the preserve of the working poor, these streets now house students and those with sufficient funds to buy what have become rather expensive cottages. This is even more

the case across Walton Street but here the preciously guarded Eden of North Oxford begins. Few settlements of less actual architectural merit could have warranted so elegiac a response from so many clever and sophisticated men and women. Barely decorated elevations in bright brick with elementary stone detailing seem at first glance seem to be a less charming and imaginative version of what is to be found in any big town. However, it is turned genuinely sublime and into a model of suburbia by the consistency of its building, the intelligent variation in size of similarly styled buildings allowing residents of wildly varying incomes to live side by side and, most of all, by a century and a half of beautiful and much adored planting that sprays a frothy blanket of cherry blossom or a blessing of waxy magnolias all over the muscular nineteenth-century houses. For all these reasons (as well as the careful street planning and generous sizes of room, stair and garden) North Oxford has survived as perhaps Britain's most beautiful suburb.

ST GILES HOUSE 1702

St GILES Closes each year in September for The St Giles fair. Roller Coasters and Ghost
brains, Candy floss and Nylon Teddies fill OXFORDS Most elegant street after Broad St
& The HIGH St

STREETS AND HOUSES

St GILES · West side

COWLEY Rd (COSMOPOLITAN OXFORD)

COWLEY Rd

St CLEMENTS *Regency Oxford*

JERICHO *Artisan Oxford*

127

RICHMOND Rd JERICHO   Enhanced Artisan with Structural polychromy.

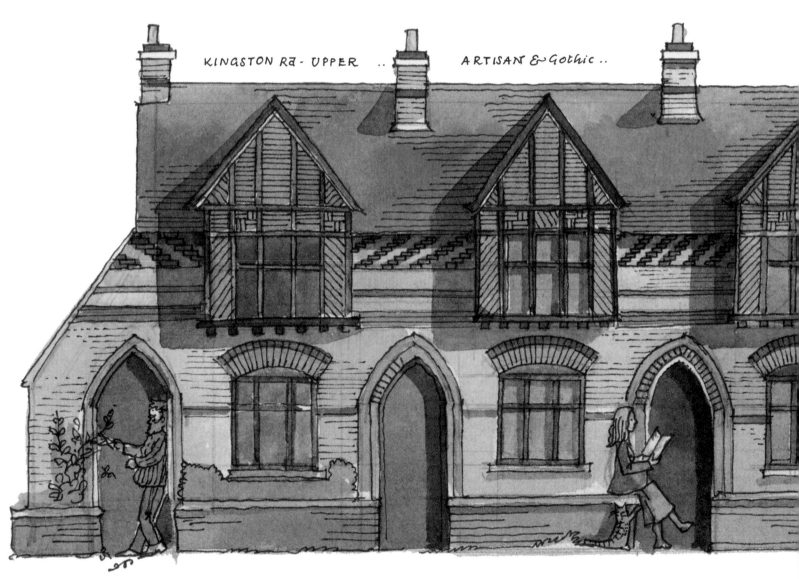

KINGSTON Rd · UPPER   ..   ARTISAN & Gothic ..

PLAYHOUSE . Reg⁑. MAUFE 1938

BEAUMONT St. GEORGIAN OXFORD 1828

ALMOST NOTHING Remains of. MEDIEVAL OXFORD. Its greatest survival until the
1970's was St Ebbes SWEPT away by The MISGUIDED OPTIMISM of the age ... This street
Was saved, all straightened out and Polished up - TRAGIC..

BLACKWELL'S BOOKSHOP founded 1879 housed in Timber framed buildings
of the C18

5 NORHAM Gardens

Nº 78 WOODSTOK Rd 1882

Nº 21 Banbury Rd · BASIL CHAMPNEYS (1842 - 1935) house of 1879
QUEEN ANNE REVIVAL

4 WINCHESTER Rd Victorian Generosity

CANTERBURY Rd

The 20th & 21st Century Suburbian developement
around Oxford have been dreary. Either with no
architectural pretensions (cowley Rd/iffley rd etc)
or in a very feeble paying of lip-service to The
N. Oxford work of moore, wilkinson et al but with
costive meaness thrown in. Imagine The pursing
of Lips and Sneering that a Poundbury, or a
Nansledan or even a Tornagrain (look them up...)
would have caused! But looking beyond The
sourfaces of the nay-sayers... How sensible to build
extensions to Oxford in an area whose high
prices would justify ARCHITECTS, IMAGINATION
HUMOUR and EFFORT. It feels like the place for it.
PERHAPS This would make good returns for the
College who instigated the Project ...and some
really good houses

Villas of the 1920/30's on the further reaches of Banbury Rd. NB: fig ⓒ is as built and ⓐ
& ⓑ have been adulterated. ⓑ is unexceptional but how PRETTY is ⓐ? - Charming and clever...
It has turned the plainest house into a Florida-Cornish Fantasy. WORTH REMEMBERING!

BANBURY RD

REGENT'S PARK COLLEGE · founded Stepney 1810
moved to Regent's park 1856 & to OXFORD 1957
1938-40 · Harold Hughes

CAUDWELL'S CASTLE (1849) on Folly Bridge
Built for a Romantic Accountant ....

©

THE BATTLE OF
THE STYLES

1835-1918

As the world's first Industrial Revolution entered its second phase, powered by steam rather than running water and with coal replacing wood as fuel, Britain perceived itself as a world power on the way to becoming the pre-eminent world power. An architectural reaction to this smoking, roaring modernity began to take shape. The mills of Northern England, the railway lines that strapped the country and the terraces of houses that sprawled ever further (and in more modest scale) around the growing industrial cities, all formed a picture that some observers found utterly repugnant. One of the most intellectually powerful of these figures turned against the present was Augustus Welby Northmore Pugin. The son of a French architectural draughtsman and painter who had fled revolutionary Paris, Auguste was soon employed by James Wyatt in the same role drawing details, furniture and elevations. Wyatt's excursions into the English Gothic may have led him to speak in the language of pinnacles, battlements and depressed perpendicular arches, but, in essence, this was still classical architecture defined by facades of repeating modules, and, above all, symmetry. Pugin longed for something quite different, a profound rethink of building that would encompass both the detailing of the old world of the pre-Renaissance and what he saw as the expression of the real nature of a building in its architecture. This was exemplified by the outward visibility of staircases which in turn promulgated a departure from symmetry in a building's elevation. With this proto-functionalism came a desire to aggressively reject the calm and resolved classical orders of Georgian Britain.

When Pugin published his slim polemic *Contrasts* in

1836, framing it as 'a return to the faith and the social structures of the Middle Ages', he set two paradigms against one another. On the one hand he portrayed an industrial city, defined by the long repetitive facades of factories and mills with tall chimney stacks and churches in the garb of what he saw as the paganism of classical Rome. And, on the other hand, he depicted a city of Gothic splendour, filled with priories and halls, spires and pinnacles. The underlying contrast was clearly set out. Pugin's argument was that preindustrial Britain, with its craftsman's guilds, chantry chapels and religious observance at its heart, was virtuous in a fundamental way that its successor was not, both in terms of spirituality and in the glorification of individual endeavour and artistic achievement. The classical style had been adopted through the industrial model. Even the blackest of wool mills might sport a pediment over its central bays, or a restrained Serlian window blackened by coaly soot. The Gothic was the language both of the virtuous old and of the future. Its adoption in intellectually advanced Oxford was both swift and whole hearted. It occurred in parallel and in partnership with the Ecclesiological movement.

The Anglican Church had atrophied during the eighteenth century. With the bright gaze of the Enlightenment drawing congregations away from a church already stripped of its mystery and medieval resonance by the Reformation even the building fell into increasing disrepair. Topographical artists may have delighted in an ivy covered tower with a traceried window peeping temptingly through the foliage, but a new breed of churchman saw only decrepitude. He also viewed the classical churches erected in Britain's growing cities as a manifestation of a departure from holiness, a kind of moral turpitude expressed in columns and pediments. The language of the ancients or, in fact, creeping secularism.

Led by powerful thinkers like John (later Cardinal) Newman this new iteration of Anglican worship was centred in Oxford and Cambridge, and it became known as the Oxford Movement. This movement stressed the centrality of the Eucharist as the focus of worship (in place of the sermon which had ruled the roost for two centuries). It was a victory for the Catholic over the Protestant factions, and, for the fabric of the church building, it meant that the altar was in the ascendancy while the hectoring pulpit was demoted to second place. Numinousness, a holiness of place, became the desirable or, indeed, essential qualification for religious architecture. The galleries, tidy box pews and decorative hatchments (those royal coats of arms on timber panels that so defined the secularisation of the church) were out and, in their place, came reminders of the long routed Catholic past: stations of the cross, reredos, sedilia, Easter sepulchre and chapels. Memorial tablets to generals and colonial officers gave way to images of the blessed Virgin Mary and, most significantly, the host (the bread or wafer) was again lifted heavenwards at the altar by a finely robed priest (attended by a full and glittering altar party, and the sound of bells and plumes of delicious smelling incense) signifying its transubstantiation from bread to the body of Christ. All this, and a whole new tradition of worship that involved a return to the medieval church (or an approximation of it) defined the mid and late nineteenth-century church and its architecture but spread beyond the ecclesiastical to the educational and beyond. Nowhere was this idea taken up with more whole hearted enthusiasm than in Oxford which was in great part built, or rebuilt, in the Gothic Revival style. While Pugin himself and his contemporary the essayist, painter and architectural theorist John Ruskin built nothing in the city, their influence was felt everywhere from the O'Shea brothers' beautiful naturalistic carving in the Natural History museum to the Italian Gothic stripes of Balliol College chapel. One of the greatest set pieces of this style was the Meadow Building at Christ Church. It is a massive edifice, containing fifty-seven sets of rooms, each with a bedroom, sitting room and study, and it takes the form of a Northern European town hall crossed with a Venetian palazzo. Structural polychromy, that is the use of real blocks of different coloured stone which are at the same time decorative and functional components of a building, is powerfully used, and the staircases are easily viewed from outside in a way that would have pleased Pugin. Vilified as hideous until the reputation of the Victorian Gothic was rescued by, among others, the painter John Piper and the poet John Betjeman, it nevertheless survived. It now serves as the backdrop for many a tourist photograph of a cutely

posing group of travellers, or of severely prosecco-exhausted post examination students.

The passion for things pointed stretched beyond the university. When in the 1850s St John's College decided to begin the development of their Walton Manor estate the initial designs were Italianate, but when the second phase, Norham Manor, was instigated in 1860 the Gothic language was adopted. Throughout the next quarter century gables, Gothic arches, simple plate tracery, oriels, turrets, heavy chimney stacks and pointed roofs came together to make North Oxford one of Britain's most atmospheric suburbs. Nineteenth-century Oxford lagged behind other towns in the Midlands in terms of commercial activity. Initially this was because of the university's power and position as a landowner, but it was also because the town had attracted none of the industrial development that stimulated the economies of nearby Birmingham, Northampton or Swindon. There was also a lack of large houses, because most of the higher status inhabitants lived in their colleges. So the gradual and careful release of building plots to the immediate north of the city led to the development of Gothic North Oxford.

CHRIST CHURCH · MEADOW BUILDING (1863~6) Thomas Deane 1828~1899
Massive and underarticulated but MUCH photographed by visitors ~ It IS impressive but has none of the grace of....

The UNIVERSITY MUSEUM · Benjamin Woodward 1816~1861 · Built
1855-9 where The larger windows (They are after all for a Museum
not undergraduate rooms) WOODWARD + Two generations of Deane
were Dublin Architects and these two buildings reflect The influence
of John RUSKIN whose 'stones of Venice' had been published in 1851.
HENCE The Elaborate wholehearted EUROPEAN GOTHIC.

WHILE EXTERNALLY GOTHIC ... INSIDE The HUGE GLASS & IRON
building, as towering as a Railway station is also GOTHIC
full of NATURALISTIC IMAGERY.. The Gallery has Column shafts
of different Marbles & stones.

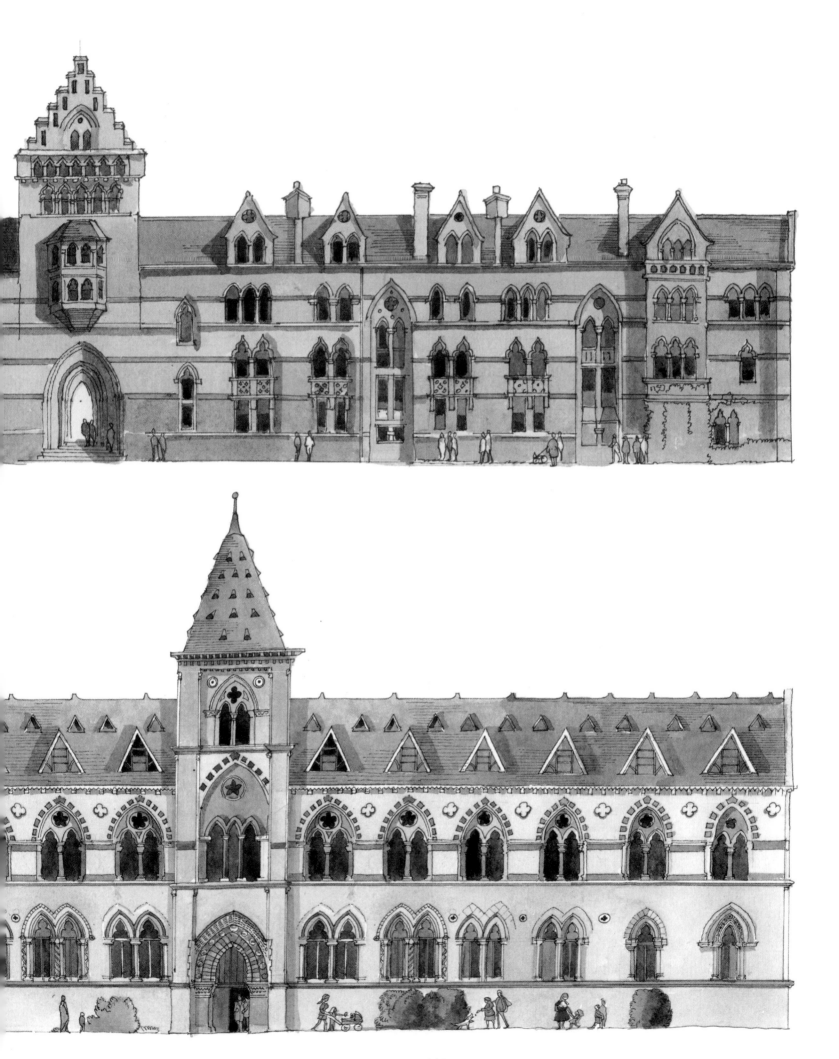

BOTH Museum & Meadow Building
are inspired by N. European town
Halls - a good NON-ECCLESIASTICAL
GOTHIC MODEL

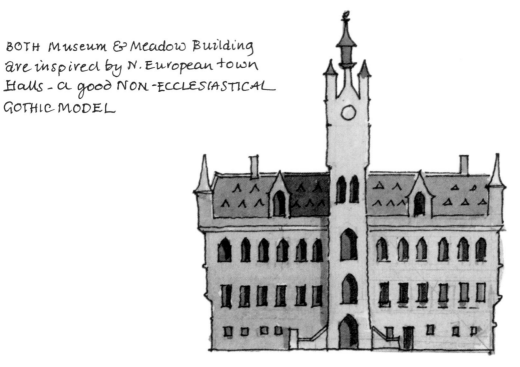

Sint Niklaas · Belgium (also G)

Bruges (The REAL Thing C. 1376)

Damme (Belgium) ALSO REAL 1464

The O'SHEA Brothers were brilliant Stone carvers coming like The Architects Woodward & Deane from DUBLIN...

MORE INSPIRATION... Pair of Windows in Oxford... The Model is in VENICE

CARVING in The UNIVERSITY MUSEUM is STYLISED in treatment but NATURALISTIC in Botanically correct SUBJECTS. The brothers worked from REAL PLANTS · This is OXALIS ⟶ Sadly funds EXPIRED and CARVING was not Completed

CROW STEPPED GABLES also of The Northern European persuasion...

AGNVS DEI · KEBLE CHAPEL

St BARNABAS 1869~72. Arthur Blomfield 1829-1899 · Anglo-Catholicism for the WORKERS...

MASS at St BARNABAS · Full POLYCHROMY - MOSAIC - STENCIL - MARBLE - GOLD - MUSIC - SMELLS ... BELLS ...

William Butterfield (1814~1900) was one
of the GREAT GOTHIC REVIVAL Architects
working most notably at Keble College
but here at BALLIOL he designed
The CHAPEL in 1857 replacing a
16 Predecessor.. Italianate bands of
Red and white masonry

St Philip and St James · WOODSTOCK Rd
1860-65 · George Edmund Street
(1824 -1881) . A Powerful building,
with Broach Spire (didn't fit in this
picture but show in Black line below
plate tracery and bands of Coloured
Stone

BROACH

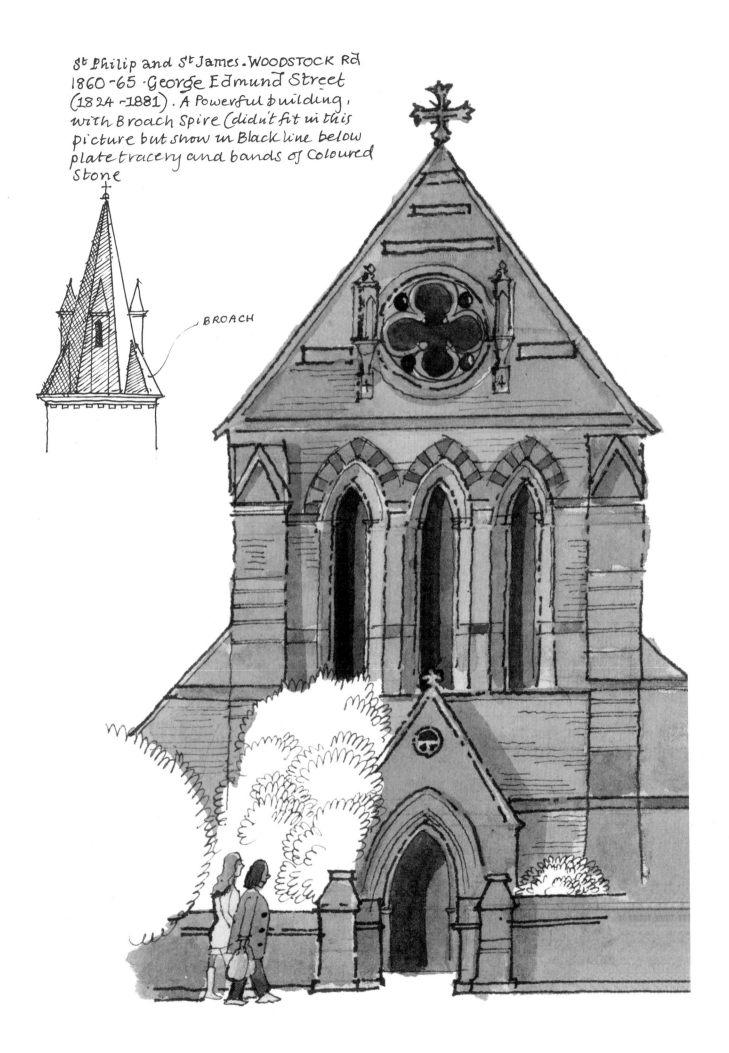

BLACKFRIARS 1929 but originally established 1221 (it became part of the university in 1994). Doran Webb was the architect 1864-1931

MAGDALEN COLLEGE. LIBRARY 1849-51 . J.C.BUCKLER 1793-10
RECENTLY U.BEAUTIFULLY RESTORED and RE-ROOFED.

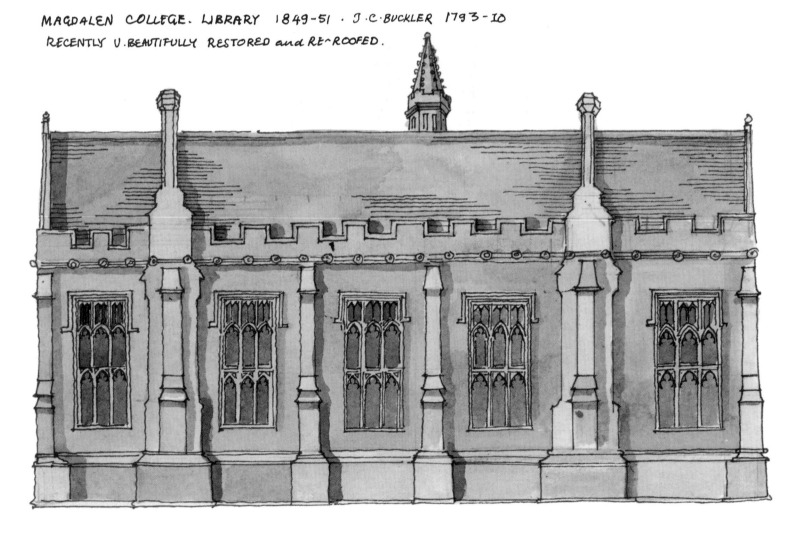

ANGEL at UNIVERSITY COLLEGE.

PUSEY HOUSE home of Anglo-Catholicom & the OXFORD MOVEMENT. 1926 ARCHITECT TEMPLE MOORE 1856~1920 with work inside the chapel by NINIAN COMPER 1864-1960..

HISTORY FACULTY. *formerly* CITY *of* OXFORD High School
for BOYS 1881. Architect T. G. JACKSON (1835~1925)
full blooded JACOBETHAN RENAISSANCE...

THE BATTLE OF THE STYLES

MANSFIELD Coll. was founded in Birmingham as a Congregationalist training Coll.
The OXFORD buildings designed by BASIL CHAMPNEYS (1842~1935)

CAMPION HALL · 1936 Edwin Lutyens (1869 ~ 1944)
The whole building is on the opposite page. It is SINGULAR
& hard to characterize beyond being STYLISH & Non-specifically
HISTORICIST...

Lodge to University Museum 1888 T.N. DEANE
(1828 - 1899) Good Hobbit Roofscape...

Lodge to UNIVERSITY PARKS 1866 H W MOORE
(1850 ~ 1915) for an austere park keeper

CAMPION HALL, BREWER St. LUTYENS

St BARNABAS SCHOOL, CLARENDEN St. G.E. STREET 1855/6

FLOOR of the CHAPEL

MASTERS LODGINGS...

KEBLE COLLEGE. 1868~82
Wm. Butterfield (1814~1900)
The great Gothic Revival masterpiece
funded in the main part by the
passionately tractarian GIBBS
family whose COLOSSAL fortune
was in part made in importing
GUANO (droppings of Cormorants,
also on part as other birds would do...)
as fertilizer for the IMPROVED
farms of (19) ENGLAND. where there's
MUCK there's BRASS. candelabra
and other decorative items for the
CELERATION of the EUCHARIST

← GUANO CORMORANT

Structural Polychromy. The use of many coloured bricks and stone in the ACTUAL BUILDING. Keble is the WORLD LEADER

LIKE St CATHERINES Coll. Keble is a <u>complete</u> WORK of ART - ie it is all built at ONE time - Stylistically opposed They are nevertheless linked in this way.

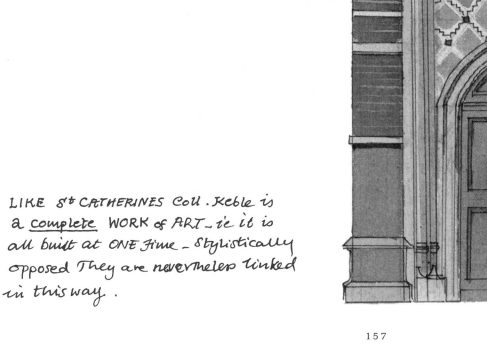

Bridge of Sighs CAMBRIDGE   1831 Architect H. Hutchinson
                                    (1800 - 1831)
                              NB. he was partner of Rickman
                              who classified the phases of
                              Engleish gothic Architecture ..

PONTE de RIALTO .VENEZIA. Antonio da Ponte 1588
he was the uncle of CONTINO ..

The 'BRIDGE of SIGHS' HERTFORD College 1914 . T G JACKSON ~ although
linked to its Venetian namesake...

....The PONTE dei' SOSPIRI... They are not alike
as much as The RIALTO.. (Cambridge similarly its own bridge!)
(FYI . Ponte dei s. ANTONIO CONTINO and built 1600)

'SMALL & POOR' was C.UFFENBACH's comment on the rather run-down Chapel at EXETER Coll in 1710. Well had he visited after 1860 he would have found Gilbert SCOTT's (1811-1878) chapel a Resplendent EXEMPLAR of the GOTHIC REVIVAL. It is built in the form of SAINTE CHAPELLE in PARIS and is ASTONISHINGLY TALL SEEMING inside and OUT.

THE BATTLE OF THE STYLES

The Whole of EXETER Coll CHAPEL

THE BATTLE OF THE STYLES

EXETER Coll Library ~ a Flourish of Medievalism.
1856 · Gilbert Scott (1811 - 1878)

N⁰ 52-4 Banbury Rd · WYCLIFFE HALL · F. CODD b. 1832
built this 1869 . Listing says "One of the BEST examples of
Victorian Gothic in N. Oxford . he was pupil of W. Wilkinson..

1903 2 Northmoor Rd · Edward Allfrey · Dutch/Queen Anne

4 WINCHESTER Rd Victorian Generosity

CIVIC PRIDE

Town and gown: the rivalry between a community and the institution with which it coexists (and which occasionally overtakes and dominates it) hit an all-time low in 1355. On the feast of St Scholastica (she was the twin sister of St Benedict which seems to have earned her a slightly minor sainthood) a fight broke out between students and a publican. The altercation became a full-scale punch-up, with the flames fanned by townspeople encouraging both sides with the war cry 'havac, havac, Smit fast, give gode knocks'. It ended with sixty-three students and thirty locals dead yet, when peace was made, it was the town that had to pay reparations. Until 1825 the mayor and corporation were obliged to process hatless to St Mary's church in order to hand over what was, by then, a token annual fine.

Later rivalries were settled in more pacific ways, not least by architectural means. The bravura flourish of Jacobean achievement that makes up the Schools and the Bodleian Library (p 73) and ends up with the show piece of the Tower of the Orders (p 72) was met by a similarly decorative manifestation of civic power. A spring in Hinksey was to provide fresh drinking water for the town and, as the central point, Carfax (where four roads joined) seemed the obvious place to put the fountain. The end of the conduit drawing water from Hinksey was marked with the pomp and dignity befitting a 'grand projet' of the city fathers in 1615. It was extravagantly decorated with four half arches supporting a domed solid lantern with niches. It is a mixture of Gothic thinking in the mode of Chichester market cross (1502) and classical pattern book detail characteristic of the halting stumble of the conversion from old (Gothic) to new (classical) ways in the Jacobean age. While the Carfax conduit was removed in

1787 it survives as a decoration in the park at nearby Nuneham House.

Despite the ever growing power and international significance of the university, Oxford, which predates it by at least five centuries, still to carry out the function of a medieval town. Walls were maintained (a few fragments remain, notably in New College) and gates (the tough Norman church tower of St Michael at the North Gate is one of them and the west of the town was dominated by the castle, where now only the moat remains). Later civic responsibilities included providing education and the city has fine examples of late nineteenth-century school buildings. The museums are an offshoot of the university but have become the second reason to visit the town. The Pitt Rivers museum is a passionate essay in Ruskinian Gothic backed up by railway station-scaled ironwork behind demonstrating the confluence of nineteenth-century industrial might and consummate craftsmanship, while the Ashmolean sounds the last brassy trumpet of classicism. In Oxford C. R. Cockerell's 1845 design of the latter building preceded the Gothic splendour of the Natural History museum by a mere decade but it is one of the previous school. Massive ionic columns, arches, cornice and pediment all say clearly that the language of learning should be that of the Ancients...

Nineteenth-century Oxford was predominantly high Anglican. The Tractarian ecclesiologist movement was fully established and there was so strong a vein of anti-Catholicism that the great A.W.N. Pugin, himself a Roman Catholic, had his plans for Balliol rejected by the Master on the grounds that a popish architect would *not* be suitable for his college. So, it was not surprising that a monument was built to the

three Protestant martyrs (Nicholas Ridley, Hugh Latimer and Thomas Cranmer) outside Balliol. All three were tried for heresy at St Mary's church and subsequently burnt at the stake in Broad Street (a cross marks the precise spot). Ridley and Latimer were burnt in 1555 and Cranmer in 1556. Giles Gilbert Scott (much in the nineteenth-century section of this book is attributed to him) was commissioned to design the memorial. It was built in the form of an Eleanor cross. These were a series of highly decorated structures erected by Edward I in memory of his wife Eleanor of Castile. The most famous version is Charing Cross in London which was rebuilt in 1863 by Charles Barry but some of the originals still remain standing. The best extant version is in Geddington in Northamptonshire and it is well worth the visit. The Oxford cross was built in 1842; it is elaborate and deeply carved. Much used as a meeting place and usually scattered with smiling tourists fiddling with their phones who are *not* remembering Ridley howling as the flames licked him 'Lord have mercy upon me, I cannot burn', or the more reassuring words of Latimer 'be of good comfort Master Ridley and play the man! We shall this day, by God's grace, light such a candle in England as I trust shall never be put out...'

Oxford Town Hall was built in 1897 and it is, in itself, quite spectacular but when compared to the stupendous shows of municipal pride in Northern cities its rather everyday Jacobethan facade in St Aldate's Street fails to compete with its more distinguished neighbour Tom Tower. Inside, however, it has powerful nineteenth-century decoration and a huge concert hall.

Oxford's industrialization was late and dominated by the Mini. William Morris (later to be made Lord Nuffield) was a maker and mender of bicycles but, in 1913, saw the possibilities of car manufacture. With initial showrooms in Longwall Street and later a grand columned showroom by Folly Bridge the business quickly grew and manufacturing took place in Cowley to the west of the city. By 1926 Morris controlled half of the British car market. The Mini was famously designed by Alec Issigonis in 1959 and they are still made today in the factory that dominates Oxford's eastern bypass.

Obvious That The GREAT MUSEUM of The GREAT UNIVERSITY TOWN should be Classical even if (in 1839) It was NOT a foregone Conclusion .. C.R.Cockerell 1783~1863. He had visited The temple of Apollo at Bassae in Greece and it was This SINGULAR ionic order that he used but Its references are many and are ROMAN as well as Greek · It is OXFORD'S LAST CLASSICAL BUILDING.

FLUTE

SHAFT

APOPHYGE (don't use this
you'll just
sound silly ..)

TORUS

Fillet

SCOTIA

PLINTH

ABACUS

VOLUTE

COCKEREL'S IONIC ORDER of BASSAE
(notes to remind you IF, you have not bought
Rice's Architectural Primer

Taylorian is part of the ENSEMBLE..

The UNIVERSITY MUSEUM (again) but then again... It's always worth another visit ~ don't miss The DODO.

Of The various classical building TYPES; Temple fronts of various styles, Theatres, Basilica, etc The TRIUMPHAL ARCH had obvious advantages . It is a ROMAN type often built to commemorate a military victory - here it is more peaceful celebrating The BOTANIC GARDEN in 1632-3 . (Nicolas Stone 1587-1647

GLORIA DEI OPT MAX   HONORI CAROLI REGIS

HENRICVS   DANBY

ASHMOLEAN / TAYLOREAN AGAIN

The ULTIMATE in 17 comfort .. CLEAN WATER . Otho Nicholson
a lawyer paid for CARFAX CONDUIT to be erected
in lavish and highly DECORATED style in
1615-17. In 1787 it was demolished and now sits
in the park of NUNEHAM COURTENAY. The fresh water
it distributed came from springs in HINKSEY well the
WELL SURVIVES. This is LATE for GOTHIC showing-off...
... a sign of OXFORD'S INNATE CONSERVATISM

CIVIC PRIDE

The Marty's memorial. Gilbert Scott
(1811~1878) was erected in 1841-2. It
Commemorates the burning of the
Protestant Martyrs CRANMER, LATIMER
& RIDLEY. Still a live issue nearly 300
years after their death...

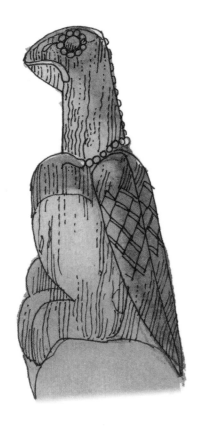

NEWEL POST in RHODES HOUSE   1929

TYMPANUM of DOOR to OXFORD Town Hall · 1893 Henry Hare in Jacobethan Style

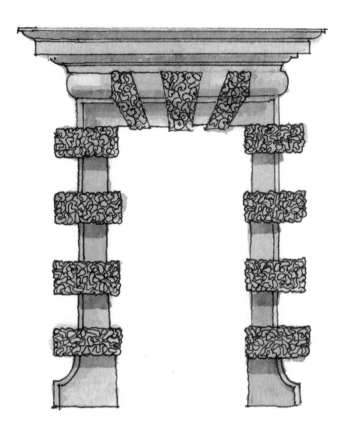

details of Magdalen BRIDGE 1790. John Gwynn (1713-1786) Architect & civil engineer

STONES ALMSHOUSES 1697 Bartholomew Peisley sr who also built St Giles House

MORRIS MOTORS Showroom 1932 .Henry Smith. Now Crown Court

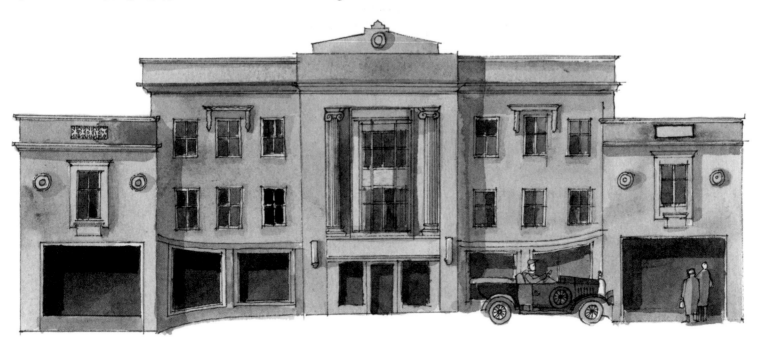

The Prize for BOLDEST PLATE Tracery in town (That is the sort that looks as if cut with a pastry cutter) goes to... The RADCLIFFE INFIRMARY (ex) Chapel 1864. Arthur Blomfield 1829-1899 N.B. same architect AND donor (T.Combe) as St BARNABAS 5 years Later.

The FIRST PUBLIC CONCERT HALL (small hall...) in EUROPE is in OXFORD... The HOLYWELL MUSIC ROOM of 1748 Arch in Thomas Camplin.

The (EX) Radcliffe Infirmary 1759 ~ 1770. Stiff Leadbetter (d.1776) a Prolific Country House Architect.

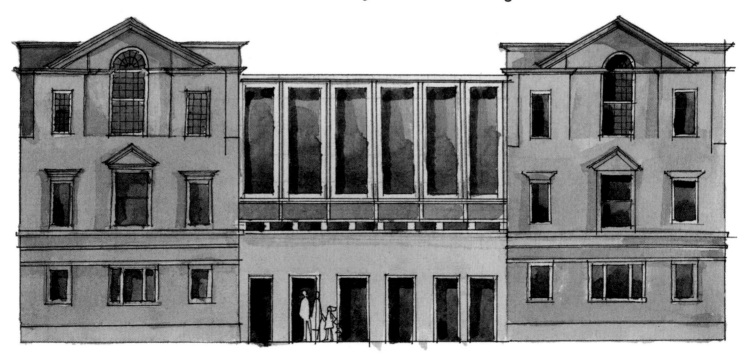

MODERN OXFORD

1945—today

Sex, the poet Philip Larkin famously claimed, was invented in 1963. The Rolling Stones (surely they knew a thing or two about this!) had been founded in 1962 and in 1961 the first man was shot into space. A year before Michael Powers of Architects' Co-Partnership had built the Beehive Building at St John's College thus pipping to the post these signals of the new age. The era of modernism in Oxford had begun. The idea that buildings should be part of a tradition, that one building or school of architecture should be the model or precedent for another, had dominated western architecture up till this time.

But the twentieth century in Oxford was far from settled in architectural taste and there was no dramatic change from the nineteenth century, when the 'battle of the styles' had raged. Classicism fought for ascendancy against the Gothic, cheered on or sharply stabbed by the second rankers: Italianate, neo-Byzantine, the deliciously and Germanically named *Rundbogenstil* (neo-Norman) and the various manifestations of the Arts and Crafts movement and the Queen Anne revival. The end of the nineteenth century and the first part of the twentieth were both still rooted, architecturally, in the past. Despite the advent of the telephone, the car, electric light and a war that totally failed to end all wars.

Maybe Oxford is extreme in that part of human nature that induces us to look FONDLY over our shoulders even when striding forward. So, in fact, despite the birth and development of modernism in Germany through the Bauhaus movement and the bright constructivist lights of Bolshevik Russia, Britain had resisted. Some bold projects had produced a few clean modern factories and a scatter-

ing of houses and offices, but it was never the mainstream architectural choice, even with the flirtatious charm of the ocean liner inspired curves of Art Deco (which took its name from the Exposition internationale des arts décoratif et industriels modernes in 1925 in Paris). Instead, a series of late historicist movements continued: there was neo-Georgian and mock-Tudor while the Arts and Crafts movement was thought to be, with its focus on function and form, in some way a precursor of the modern. Oxford took a particular interest in the latter style and the use of rough cut Cotswold stone walling, sometimes on a scale or to an extent that made madness of the vernacular prevents as in the building of the Weston Library. The great English architect of the Edwardian era was Sir Edwin Lutyens famous for the viceregal and government buildings in Delhi and Castle Drogo in Devon (1930). In Oxford, Lutyens produced Campion Hall in Brewer Street in 1936 and its bold, unfussy elevation is a powerful contrast to its surroundings. At the other end of town is Lady Margaret Hall with its great Wolfson Quadrangle designed by the twentieth-century classicist Raymond Erith. Restrained, austere and dignified, it forms an interesting contrast with John Simpson's rather more bombastic lodges and screens to the same college, which also has a chapel by Giles Gilbert Scott.

International modernism did, however, finally arrive in Oxford and it is at its most stylish in Wolfson College, an extravagant essay in beautiful and unusually detailed concrete by Powell & Moya, and in the extraordinarily complete work of art that is St Catherine's College. Here in 1959 this forward-looking college commissioned the

Danish architect Arne Jacobsen to produce complete designs for a modern college as all encompassing as any medieval monastery. Now with canals and lawns, grand informal planting and populated by geese and ducks as well as members, it feels as architecturally established as Merton or Magdalen and it is as interesting to walk round as either. Jacobsen's work stretches beyond the architectural to the furniture (notably the famously uncomfortable dining chairs) and on to the stylish cutlery used in a Hall that is, despite its modernist clothing, a pure and clear re-reading of the essential tradition of Oxford architecture. New building continues in colleges and in the university. The Blavatnik School of Government in Walton Street sends an incomprehensible but nevertheless stylish ocean liner's prow probing out towards the grand screen of the Oxford University Press. Around it the old hospital site has a series of big new buildings, a Windy City in the heart of Oxford saved, as most of the city's building over the centuries has been, by a higher than average spend per square metre allowing quality to creep in to even the least inspired grand plan.

The near Stalinist megalomaniacal Saïd Business School saves the touchingly newly named Frideswide Square from winning the prize for most bathetic entrance to any great city. The station (sadly poor and commercial work of 1974) greets visitors and sends them on an initially underwhelming walk into town but perhaps this is merely a tempting veil thrown over the head of a great beauty. A warning – a competition for a new station was recently held throwing up a series of schemes, any of which that might induce the unthinkable: nostalgia for the current building. Something, perhaps, for the next edition...

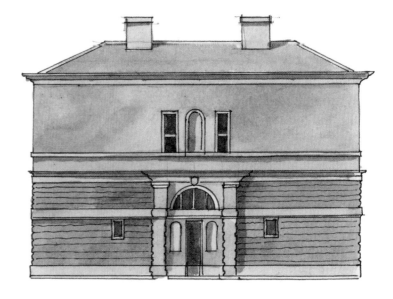

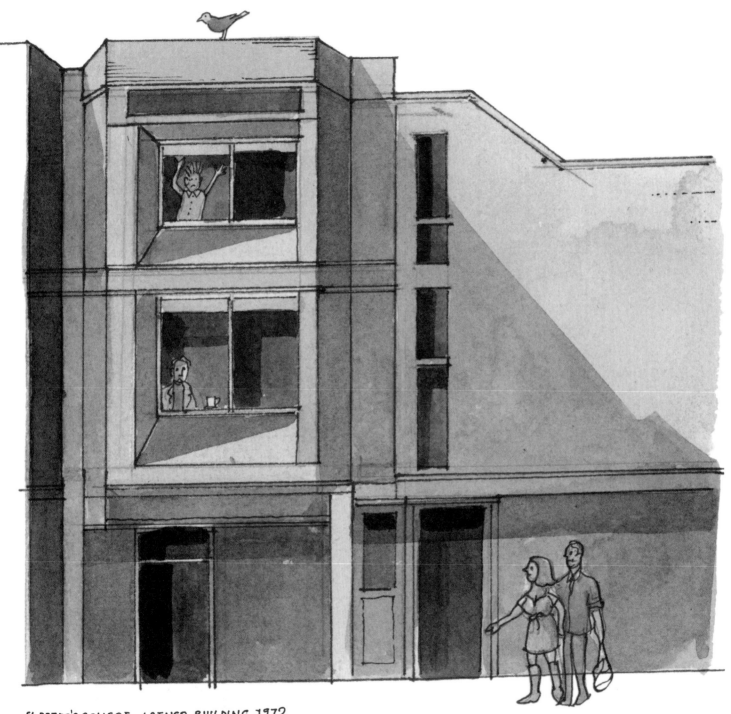

St PETER'S COLLEGE LATNER BUILDING 1972
KENNETH STEVENS & ASSOCIATES.

SOMERVILLE College · FRY BUILDING 1967 · Arup Associates · Philip DOWSON
once STARTLING now DISTINGUISHED .. A PERIOD PIECE with CONCRETE AGEING V. WELL .

ST EDMUND HALL - KELLY BUILDING. GABLED TOPS OF 6 BAYS to RHS REFER To TIMBER framed Town HOUSES NEARBY. TOWER (V TALL) has STAIRS & No LIFT...

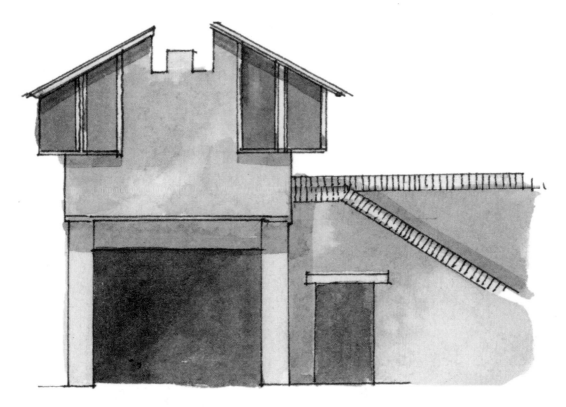

LODGE at North entrance to WORCESTER College   Richard MacCormac (1938 ~ 2014)

St JOHN's COLLEGE · BEEHIVE BUILDING 1960 · MICHAEL POWERS of ARCHITECTS' CO PARTNERSHIP
The first Great Modernist Triumph in OXFORD. HIGHEST SPEC' in PORTLAND STONE ETC

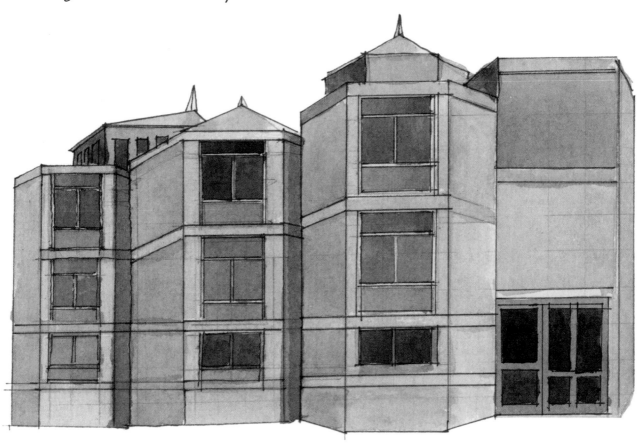

St Anthony's College 1968 Howell, Killick, Partridge & Amis

WOLFSON COLLEGE. POWELL & MOYA 1965

WOLFSON College 1969-74 POWELL & MOYA. FRUITY-BRUTALISM with BAROQUE VERMICULATION & IMPORTANTLY Built to a v HIGH SPEC. Similar blocks in deprived urban areas fared LESS WELL. --

GENUINELY <u>ODD</u> Tower (and gate)
at HARRIS MANCHESTER · 2014
YIANGOU ARCHITECTS · Too big?
too small? Somehow STRANGE
& with contemporary Inscriptions.
EXCITING though, that it was BUILT

MODERN OXFORD

NUFFIELD COLLEGE 1949 . AUSTEN HARRISON 1891~1976
a COMPLETE SCHEME but perhaps SLIGHTLY lacking in HUMOUR
but with a CRACKING TOWER & COPPER SPIRE that GREETS
Train travellers to OXFORD PROPER

Lady Margaret Hall · 2 Lodges and a screen · J. SIMPSON 2017 .
Classical order imposed with muscularity on Suburban N. Oxford...

L·M·H· Wolfson QUAD · 1961 Raymond Erith (1904 ~ 1973)
restrained Georgian amongst the muddle...

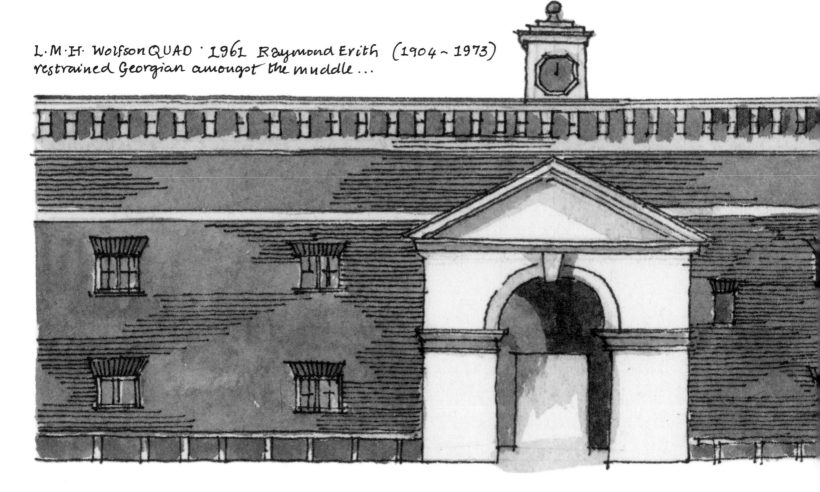

RESTRAINED NEO-CLASSICAL at MAGDALEN
with ACROTERIA

WILD PUEBLO HISPANO-JACOBEAN at St ANNES
with Beavers

The SACKLER Library. St John's St · 2001 · Robert Adam architects
BRAVE COMMISIONING of a major NEOCLASSICAL BUILDING and in a GEORGIAN St
PHEN!

QUEEN'S COLLEGE · PROVOSTS LODGINGS 1958 · RAYMOND ERITH 1904 ·'73
RESTRAINED AND
MASTERFUL.

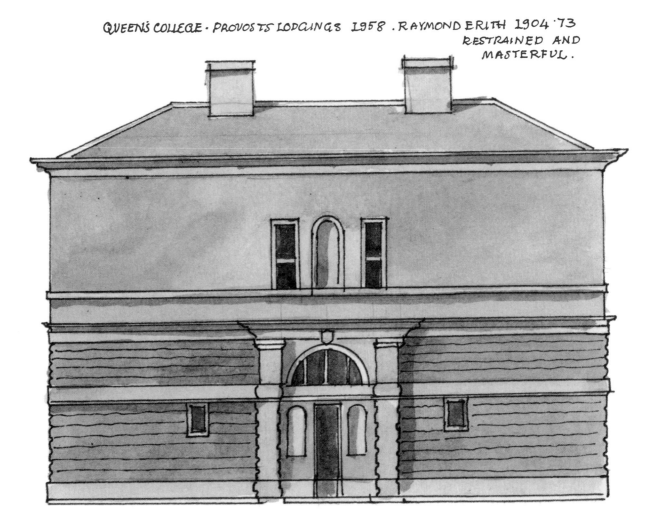

St CATHERINES Coll. 1964 Arne JACOBSEN 1902~1971 . The uncompromisingly MODERN College..
AND ELEGANT & REFINED...

St HILDA'S COll · Restrained C20

St HUGH'S COLL - more full blooded
Queen Anne Revival · 1914 ·

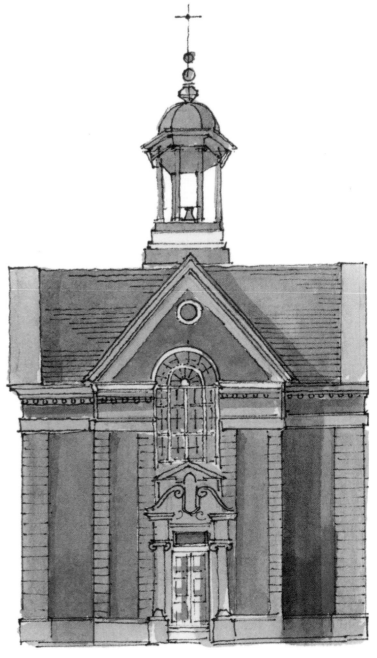

INDEX

ACKNOWLEDGEMENTS

In writing the very short text and drawing the huge number of pictures in this book I have received help and advice from those with proper knowledge and real brains; Professors John Blair and Otto Saumerez Smith, Drs Edward Impey, Anna Keay and Simon Thurley, Rev Jonathan Beswick, Alastair Langlands and other kind people.

I have received encouragement from my other friends especially Kate Harris, Jackie Rose, Andy Paddick, Talulah Riley, The St Barnabas choir, Becky Craven and Nell Stroud and received real hands on assistance from Josh Hale, Lucian Robinson, Will Whitaker and my wonderful assistant Charlotte Pile.

I am grateful to the patient team at White Lion, Nicki Davis, Glenn Howard, Joe Hallsworth and Andrew Dunn who commissioned the book and Caroline Dawnay my agent.

Most of all it was Emma Bridgewater who brought me to Oxford, something about which I have been peculiarly graceless for which, and in print, I apologise.

First published in 2019 by White Lion Publishing,
an imprint of The Quarto Group.

The Old Brewery, 6 Blundell Street
London, N7 9BH,
United Kingdom
T (0)20 7700 6700
www.QuartoKnows.com

A catalogue record for this book is available from the
British Library.

ISBN 978 0 71123 932 6
Ebook ISBN 978 0 71124 720 8

10 9 8 7 6 5 4 3 2 1

Printed in China

Brimming with creative inspiration, how-to projects and useful information
to enrich your everyday life, Quarto Knows is a favourite destination for those
pursuing their interests and passions. Visit our site and dig deeper with our
books into your area of interest: Quarto Creates, Quarto Cooks, Quarto Homes,
Quarto Lives, Quarto Drives, Quarto Explores, Quarto Gifts, or Quarto Kids.